Reptiles

The Nature Company Discoveries Library published by Time-Life Books

Conceived and produced by
Weldon Owen Pty Limited
43 Victoria Street, McMahons Point,
NSW, 2060, Australia
A member of the
Weldon Owen Group of Companies
Sydney • San Francisco
Copyright © 1996 US Weldon Owen Inc.
Copyright © 1996 Weldon Owen Pty Ltd
Reprinted 1997

THE NATURE COMPANY
Priscilla Wrubel, Ed Strobin, Steve Manning,
Georganne Papac, Tracy Fortini

TIME-LIFE BOOKS
Time-Life Books is a division of Time Life Inc.
Time-Life is a trademark of Time Warner Inc.
U.S.A.

Time-Life Custom Publishing
Vice President and Publisher: Terry Newell
Director of New Product Development:
Quentin McAndrew
Managing Editor: Donia Ann Steele
Director of Sales: Neil Levin
Director of Financial Operations: J. Brian Birky

WELDON OWEN Pty Limited
Chairman: Kevin Weldon
President: John Owen
Publisher: Sheena Coupe
Managing Editor: Rosemary McDonald
Project Editor: Kathy Gerrard
Text Editor: Claire Craig
Art Director: Sue Burk
Designer: Karen Clarke
Assistant Designer: Angela Pelizzari
Visual Research Coordinator: Jenny Mills

Photo Research: Annette Crueger
Illustration Research: Peter Barker
Production Manager: Caroline Webber
Production Assistant: Kylie Lawson
Vice President, International Sales:
Stuart Laurence
Coeditions Director: Derek Barton

Text: Carson Creagh

Illustrators: Anne Bowman; Simone End;
Christer Eriksson; John Francis/Bernard Thornton
Artists, UK; Robert Hynes; David Kirshner;
Frank Knight; James McKinnon;
Colin Newman/Bernard Thornton Artists, UK;
Peter Schouten; Trevor Ruth; Rod Westblade

Library of Congress
Cataloging-in-Publication Data
Reptiles / Carson Creagh

    p. cm. -- (Discoveries Library)

    Includes index.
    ISBN 0-8094-9247-4

    1. Reptiles--Juvenile literature. [1. Reptiles.]
    I. Title. II. Series

    QL644.2.C68 1996
    597.96--dc20   95-24477

Printed in China

A Weldon Owen Production

THE NATURE COMPANY
DISCOVERIES
L I B R A R Y

Reptiles

CONSULTING EDITOR

Dr. Allen E. Greer

Principal Research Scientist,
The Australian Museum,
Sydney, Australia

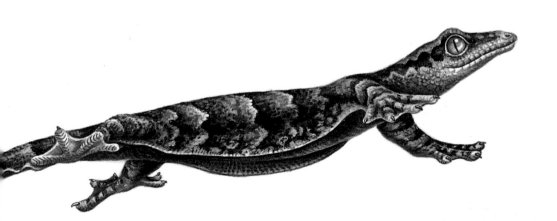

TIME
LIFE
BOOKS

Contents

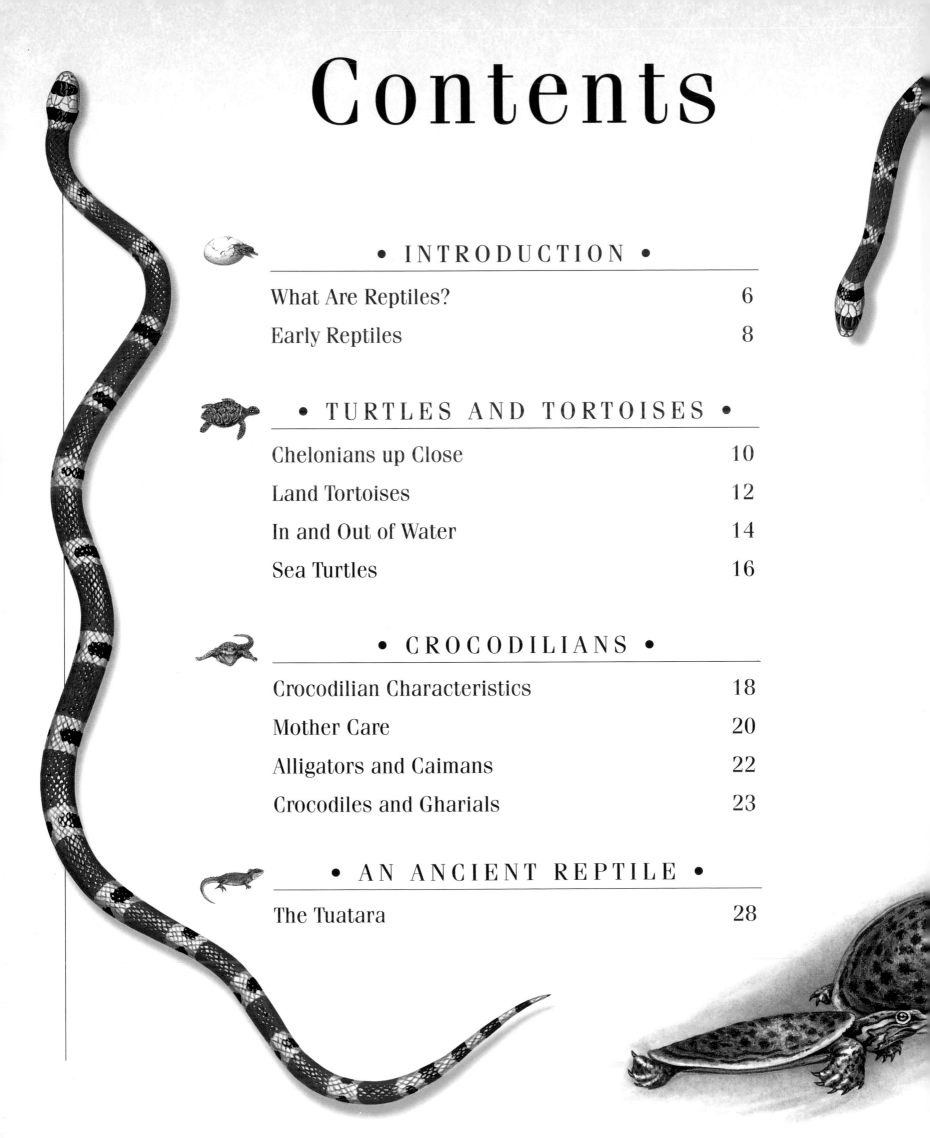

What Are Reptiles?

SOAKING UP THE SUN
A crocodilian stretches out to absorb heat from the sun so it has energy to hunt later in the day. Warm-blooded animals, such as birds and mammals, generate heat inside their own bodies.

Reptiles have existed for millions of years. Their ancestors were amphibians that lived on land and in water. Unlike their ancestors, however, reptiles have tough skins and their eggs have shells. These adaptations allowed them to break away from water and evolve into a variety of types living in many environments. The four orders of living reptiles are the chelonians (turtles and tortoises), crocodilians (crocodiles, alligators, caimans and gharials), rhynchocephalians (tuataras) and squamates (lizards and snakes). They vary in size and structure, but they all have features in common. They are usually found on land, and they are vertebrates (animals with bony skeletons and central backbones, as shown left). Their skin is covered with scutes or scales to protect them from predators and rough ground. Reptiles are cold-blooded and depend on the sun and warm surfaces to heat their bodies.

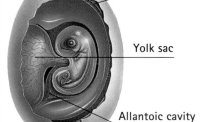

PARTNERS
Reptiles' eggs are fertilized inside the females by males. Amphibians, however, fertilize their eggs outside the body. Water carries the sperm to the eggs.

Chorion

Yolk sac

Allantoic cavity

WONDERFUL EGG
Oxygen, which helps the embryo to grow, enters the egg through the chorion, just beneath the eggshell. The yolk sac nourishes the embryo, and waste is stored in the allantoic cavity.

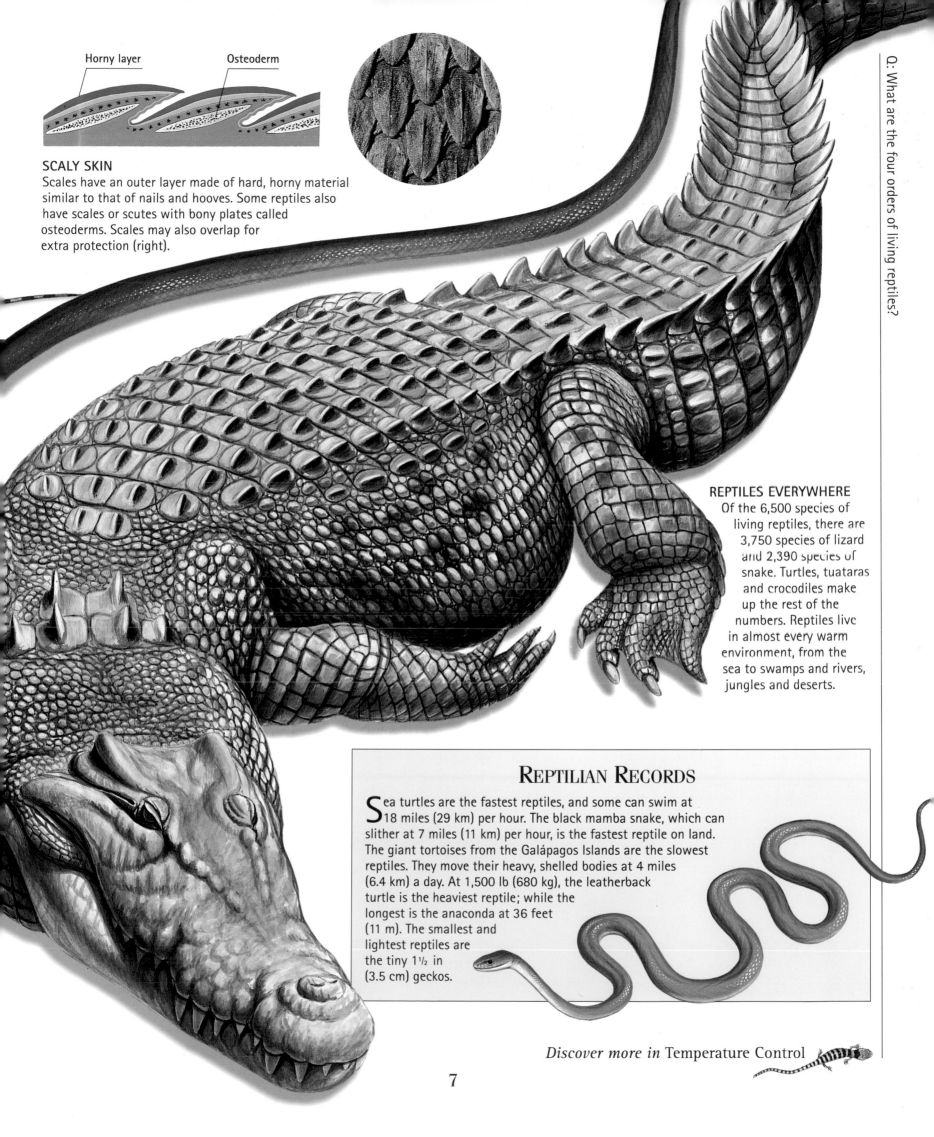

Horny layer   Osteoderm

SCALY SKIN
Scales have an outer layer made of hard, horny material similar to that of nails and hooves. Some reptiles also have scales or scutes with bony plates called osteoderms. Scales may also overlap for extra protection (right).

REPTILES EVERYWHERE
Of the 6,500 species of living reptiles, there are 3,750 species of lizard and 2,390 species of snake. Turtles, tuataras and crocodiles make up the rest of the numbers. Reptiles live in almost every warm environment, from the sea to swamps and rivers, jungles and deserts.

REPTILIAN RECORDS
Sea turtles are the fastest reptiles, and some can swim at 18 miles (29 km) per hour. The black mamba snake, which can slither at 7 miles (11 km) per hour, is the fastest reptile on land. The giant tortoises from the Galápagos Islands are the slowest reptiles. They move their heavy, shelled bodies at 4 miles (6.4 km) a day. At 1,500 lb (680 kg), the leatherback turtle is the heaviest reptile; while the longest is the anaconda at 36 feet (11 m). The smallest and lightest reptiles are the tiny 1½ in (3.5 cm) geckos.

Discover more in Temperature Control

Coelurosauravus, 16 in (40 cm) long, from the late Permian Period, could glide from tree to tree like a flying lizard today.

A LIVING REPTILE
The Indopacific, or saltwater, crocodile is a giant among today's reptiles, but many extinct reptiles were much larger.

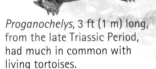

Although 10-ft (3-m) long *Dimetrodon* from the Permian Period was a reptile, it was also related to the ancestors of mammals.

Hylonomus, 8 in (20 cm) long, from the Carboniferous Period, is known only from fossils found trapped in fossilized tree trunks.

Proganochelys, 3 ft (1 m) long, from the late Triassic Period, had much in common with living tortoises.

• INTRODUCTION •

Early Reptiles

The first amphibians crawled out of the water about 400 million years ago to take advantage of the new habitats available on land. But they still had to lay their jellylike eggs in water. About 300 million years ago, during the Carboniferous Period, some of these animals developed eggs with a waterproof shell that protected the growing young from drying out. The young inside these eggs had a much better chance of surviving on land, and new species began to evolve. The earliest known reptile was *Hylonomus*, and it looked like a small lizard. Later reptiles included pterosaurs, plesiosaurs, dinosaurs, lizards, snakes, crocodiles, turtles and tuataras, which lived during the Age of Reptiles (250 to 65 million years ago). Dinosaurs died out after dominating the land for 150 million years, but the ancestors of today's reptiles survived to evolve into thousands of different species.

AN EXTINCT REPTILE
Scientists study fossil reptiles, such as the dinosaur fossil above, and compare them with living reptiles. Such research can tell scientists much about the bodies of ancient reptiles and the way they lived.

SMALL BEGINNINGS
The outlines shown here are the reptiles from the main illustration. Pterosaurs, dinosaurs, ichthyosaurs and plesiosaurs died out in the Cretaceous Period, but the surviving reptiles went on to evolve into 6,500 species of living reptile.

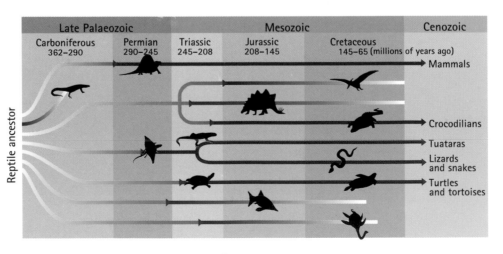

	Late Palaeozoic			Mesozoic		Cenozoic
	Carboniferous 362–290	Permian 290–245	Triassic 245–208	Jurassic 208–145	Cretaceous 145–65 (millions of years ago)	

Reptile ancestor

Mammals

Crocodilians

Tuataras

Lizards and snakes

Turtles and tortoises

Evolving

Living

Dying out

Q: Which reptiles lived during the Age of Reptiles?

Pteranodon, a pterosaur from the late Cretaceous Period, had a 23-ft (7-m) wingspan. It fed on fish like a modern pelican.

Pachyrachis, 3 ft (1 m) long, from the early Cretaceous Period, may be related to the ancestor of today's snakes.

Stegosaurus, 30 ft (9 m) long, from the late Jurassic Period, was a dinosaur that ate plants, just like an iguana.

Planocephalosaurus, 8 in (20 cm) long, from the late Triassic Period, resembled the New Zealand tuatara.

LIVING IN A NEW WORLD

Amphibians are the ancestors of reptiles. There are some similarities between amphibians and reptiles, but their differences are much more important. Amphibians (their name means "living in two worlds") cannot survive far from a moist environment. They lay their eggs in water, and their young go through a larval stage in water. Reptiles, however, can live in dry places. Their eggs have a shell that prevents the baby reptile from drying out.

Deinosuchus, from the Cretaceous Period, may have grown to 49 ft (15 m) long. It could be the largest crocodile ever to have lived.

Archelon, 12 ft (3.7 m) long, from the late Cretaceous Period, may have fed on jellyfish like a leatherback turtle.

Elasmosaurus, a 46-ft (14-m) long plesiosaur, from the late Cretaceous Period, had the longest neck of any marine reptile.

Ichthyosaurus, 7 ft (2 m) long, from the early Jurassic Period, was streamlined and ate fish, like a living dolphin.

9

Chelonians up Close

TOP LAYER
The layer of horny plates, or scutes, that covers the carapace and plastron is made of a material called keratin—the same substance as the outer layer of your fingernails.

BONY LAYER
The radiated tortoise has striking patterns on its high-domed, heavy shell. The shell is fused to the spine and ribs of the tortoise. The upper shell is called the carapace; the lower shell is called the plastron.

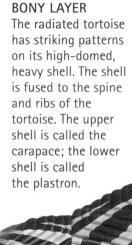

Chelonians, or tortoises and turtles, appeared more than 200 million years ago and have changed very little since then. They are the only reptiles with bony shells as part of their skeletons. Many can pull their heads and legs inside their shells, making it difficult for predators to eat them. Living chelonians are divided into two groups according to the way they draw their heads into their shells. The 200 or so species of straight-necked turtle, freshwater and semi-terrestrial (semi-land) turtle and tortoise have flexible necks that they can pull back (retract) straight into their shells. The 60 or so species of side-necked turtle, which live in Africa, South America and Australia, bend their necks sideways and curl their heads under the front of their upper shell. A chelonian's shell varies in shape, color and hardness. The shape of the shell tells us much about how chelonians move and the different environments in which they live (as shown in the shells below). All chelonians lay eggs, which they usually bury in a hole dug in the sand or earth.

Scute

BREAKING FREE
Chelonians fend for themselves as soon as they hatch. They use a sharp bump (which drops off) on top of the snout to break free of their leathery shells.

Land tortoise
Domed shell, slow moving

Semi-terrestrial turtle
Flattened shell for land and water

Pond turtle
Small, flattened shell

DINING ON DAISIES
Sea turtles eat shellfish, fish, jellyfish and seagrasses. Young land tortoises eat worms and insects as well as plants. Adult tortoises, which move too slowly to catch prey, eat flowers, fruit and plants.

THE LONG AND THE SHORT OF IT

A side-necked turtle has a long neck and a flattened shell. It has to turn its head to one side (below left), perhaps because it does not have enough space inside the shell to pull its head back into it. Most straight-necked turtles and tortoises have shorter necks and can easily retract their heads (below right). Straight-necked tortoises with long necks, such as the giant tortoises of the Aldabra and Galápagos islands, have plenty of room inside their large, domed shells to retract their necks.

Retracting neck

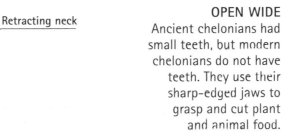

OPEN WIDE
Ancient chelonians had small teeth, but modern chelonians do not have teeth. They use their sharp-edged jaws to grasp and cut plant and animal food.

Land tortoise

SUITABLE LIMBS
Chelonians' legs have evolved to suit different environments. Land tortoises have column-shaped legs with claws. Pond turtles need to move on land and in the water, so they have webbing between their claws. Sea turtles have flippers to propel them through the water.

Carapace

Plastron

Sea turtle
Streamlined shell for swimming

Pond turtle

Sea turtle

Land Tortoises

Many land tortoises live in dry environments or deserts. Most have high-domed shells to protect them from predators and perhaps to provide room for larger lungs. As their shells are very strong and heavy, land tortoises are slow moving—the most they could move in an hour would be about 295 ft (90 m)—and use very little energy. In hot areas, they are active only in the morning and late afternoon. They lie in the shade of shrubs and trees or in burrows in the soil during the blistering heat of the day. There are about 40 species of land tortoise, and they can be found in Asia, Africa, Europe, and North and South America. Most species are plant eaters, though some also eat insects and snails. The larger land tortoises can live for 100 years or more, but many species, especially those that live on islands, are endangered. Pigs and rats eat both eggs and young tortoises.

KEEPING COOL
The desert-dwelling gopher tortoise digs a burrow and retreats into it during the heat of the day and the cold of winter.

LITTLE AND LARGE
Land tortoises range in size from the 4-in (10-cm) long Madagascan spider tortoises to the 8-in (20-cm) long South American tortoises and the wheelbarrow-sized giants of the Aldabra and Galápagos islands.

A NARROW FIT
The African pancake tortoise lives among rocks. Unlike other land tortoises, which usually have domed shells, it has a flattened, slightly soft shell so that it can squeeze into narrow crevices for protection.

LAYING TIME
Land tortoises lay their eggs in nests scraped out of the soil. Like all chelonians, they leave the eggs. The hatchlings must look after themselves.

DID YOU KNOW?
For many years, sailing ships on long voyages across the Pacific Ocean stopped at the Galápagos Islands to collect giant tortoises. The sailors killed the tortoises when they needed fresh meat.

DIFFERENT SHELLS

When populations of tortoises were isolated from each other on the Galápagos Islands many thousands of years ago, each group adapted to different conditions. Tortoises on the large, wetter islands are called domes because they have developed big, domelike shells (below). Tortoises on the smaller, drier islands, where plants grow tall, have long legs and a smaller "saddleback" shell. This is raised in front so the tortoises can stretch their necks up to reach cactus leaves.

SADDLEBACK STRETCH

In dry times, giant saddleback tortoises get water and food from tall cactus plants. But when it does rain, dozens of tortoises collect around puddles and drink as much as they can.

In and Out of Water

Most chelonians live in or near fresh water such as lakes, rivers, swamps and estuaries. There are 200 or so species of freshwater turtle, from pond turtles, softshell turtles, mud and musk turtles to river turtles. Almost all of these have webbed feet with claws, and light, flat shells covered with horny plates. Many of them take in oxygen from the water as well as from the air. Most freshwater turtles lay their eggs in soil or in sandy river banks—the Australian northern snake-necked turtle is the only chelonian to lay its eggs underwater. They ambush their prey of aquatic insects and fish underwater and can stay submerged for long periods (some species hibernate underwater for weeks). Semi-terrestrial (living both in water and on land) turtles are closely related to freshwater turtles. They hunt on land as well as in the water, and eat both plant and animal food. Semi-terrestrial species may hibernate in the mud underwater or in burrows and holes on land.

VACUUM MEALS
The mata-mata is a freshwater turtle from South America. It sucks up prey with its wide mouth.

BIG HEAD
The Asian big-headed turtle spends most of its time in water, where it hunts like a snapping turtle by ambushing prey.

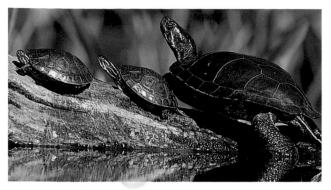

SOFTSHELL TURTLES
Three families of turtles lack horny plates. The largest of these families, the softshell turtles, have flat shells and leathery skin. They are fast swimmers and can hide from predators on the bottom of muddy ponds.

WARMING UP
Like all reptiles, turtles are cold-blooded. These pond turtles soak up warmth (energy) from the sun before they set off to hunt for food in cool water.

MAKE IT SNAPPY
The alligator snapping turtle is camouflaged by a muddy brown shell and skin, and by algae growing on its shell. It waves its wormlike tongue to lure fish into its strong jaws, which could easily bite off your finger.

LOVE DANCE
As male and female turtles usually look the same, they recognize each other through behavior rather than by appearance. Male turtles bite or head-butt females, or "dance" in the water to attract a female's attention. During the spring breeding season, this male red-eared turtle courts a female by fluttering his claws in front of her face.

TUCKING IN
The ornate box turtle lives in the woodlands of North America. It draws its head and legs into its domed shell to protect itself from predators and from drying out.

17

Sea Turtles

DEEP DIVER
The leatherback turtle can dive to 1,000 ft (300 m). Some leatherbacks die when they choke on plastic bags, which they think are jellyfish.

The seven species of sea turtle have flattened, streamlined shells and large front flippers. They can swim at speeds of up to 18 miles (29 km) per hour when they are escaping from predators such as sharks. Usually, they swim much more slowly, using the ocean currents to help them search for food. They eat fish, jellyfish, sponges, seagrasses, crabs—and sometimes floating garbage, which they mistake for food. Some sea turtles spend most of their lives wandering tropical oceans and traveling thousands of miles. They mate for the first time when they are several years old. Each year, the turtles return to the same beach (often great distances away from their feeding grounds) to breed. The females scoop deep holes where they lay up to 100 eggs at a time. Even though sea turtles produce many young, these hatchlings have a perilous life and few survive to become adults. Adult turtles also face many hazards. They often become tangled in fishing nets and drown. Some, such as the green, flatback, hawksbill and leatherback turtles, are killed for food or their shells.

RACE TO THE SEA

Hatching is the most dangerous time for a flatback turtle. Guided by the low, open horizon, newborn flatbacks race to the sea, relying on safety in numbers to help them escape from predators such as birds and crabs. Some reach the sea, but even then they are not safe. Sharks and other fish patrol the shallow waters, ready to eat the hatchlings. Scientists estimate that only one turtle in 100 will live to become an adult.

STRANGE BUT TRUE

Folk tales tell of sea turtles crying when they leave the ocean. In fact, sea turtles, such as this loggerhead, "cry" to get rid of salt. Special glands close to the eyes produce salty "tears" all the time. These tears are washed away when the turtles are in the water, so we can see them only when the turtles are on land.

WITH ALL THEIR MIGHT
Green turtles swim gracefully in the ocean but move clumsily on land as they haul themselves slowly onto the sand to lay their eggs.

OCEAN GIANTS
Most sea turtles return to the beaches where they hatched to mate and nest. Sea turtles such as these olive ridleys mate offshore from the nesting beach.

DANGER IN SIGHT
Hawksbill turtles are endangered because the scutes (the large scales of their carapaces) can be turned into luxury tortoiseshell items such as eyeglass frames.

17

Crocodilian Characteristics

Crocodilians are some of the world's largest and most dangerous living reptiles. Lying submerged, with only their eyes, ears and nostrils showing, these fierce predators attack with a sudden rush, surprising an antelope drinking at the river's edge or even a bird roosting above the water. The 12 species of crocodile, one dwarf crocodile, one tomistoma, one gharial, two alligators and five caimans can be found in tropical regions around the world. The biggest species, the Indopacific or saltwater crocodile, can grow to 23 ft (7 m), and has been seen swimming in the open ocean, 620 miles (1,000 km) from land. Crocodilians eat everything from insects, frogs and snails to fish, turtles and birds. Some large crocodilians even eat mammals as big as horses and cattle. Crocodilians are cold-blooded, but many species control their temperature by their behavior. An adult Nile crocodile, for example, basks in the sun on a river bank during the day. But at night, as the temperature drops, it retreats to the warmer water.

DID YOU KNOW?

Crocodilians have hundreds of teeth during their lives—but not all at the same time. Crocodilians break or lose their teeth constantly when they hunt. New teeth grow to replace the broken or missing ones.

BRIGHT SHINING EYES
Crocodilians have well-developed eyesight. They can probably see color, and their eyes have a reflective area at the back to help them see at night.

BIG AND SMALL
Crocodilians vary in size. Cuvier's dwarf caiman is 5 ft (1.5 m) when fully grown and is the smallest crocodilian. The tomistoma is a medium-sized crocodilian, but it is only about half the length of the enormous Indopacific or saltwater crocodile.

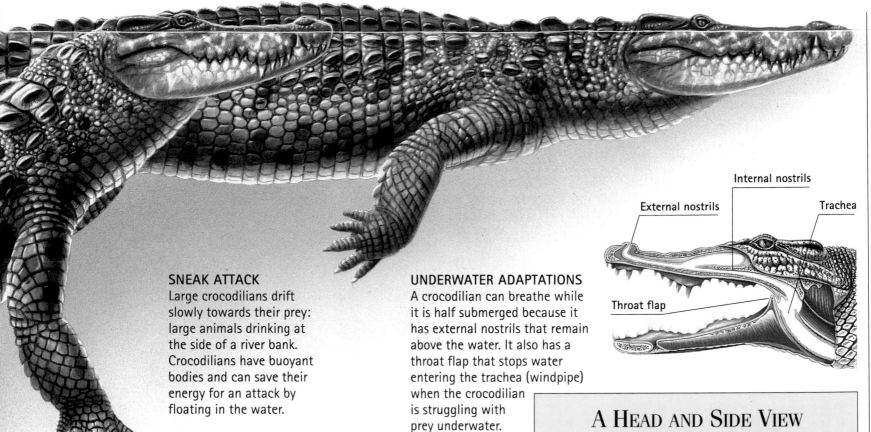

SNEAK ATTACK
Large crocodilians drift slowly towards their prey: large animals drinking at the side of a river bank. Crocodilians have buoyant bodies and can save their energy for an attack by floating in the water.

UNDERWATER ADAPTATIONS
A crocodilian can breathe while it is half submerged because it has external nostrils that remain above the water. It also has a throat flap that stops water entering the trachea (windpipe) when the crocodilian is struggling with prey underwater.

Internal nostrils

External nostrils

Trachea

Throat flap

A HEAD AND SIDE VIEW

Crocodilian snouts vary in shape and size, according to their diets and the way they live.

Crocodiles' snouts are usually pointed. When crocodiles close their mouths, the fourth tooth in the lower jaw is still visible.

American crocodile

Alligators and caimans mostly have broad snouts. Species with broader snouts eat larger prey. When alligators and caimans close their mouths, the fourth tooth of the lower jaw is not visible.

Black caiman

Gharials have long, narrow snouts and many small, pointed teeth, which they use to grasp slippery fish.

Gharial

MESSY EATERS
Crocodilians' teeth are designed to grip, not cut. Because they cannot chew their food, they swallow prey whole or tear it into large pieces.

ON LAND
On mud banks, crocodilians slide on their stomachs. For longer distances, they walk on their short legs, carrying their bellies off the ground. Some species, such as the common caiman, can walk for many miles in search of new hunting territories.

Discover more in Crocodiles and Gharials

Mother Care

Crocodilians are some of the most ferocious reptiles in the world, but female crocodilians look after their eggs and young more carefully than most reptiles. Some species make nests by scraping soil and vegetation into mounds; others bury their eggs in holes in the sand or soil. In South America, Schneider's dwarf caimans make nests in shady rainforests. As there is no heat from the sun to warm the eggs, the female builds a nest beside a termite mound by scraping together plant material, which she then uses to cover the eggs. Heat from the rotting vegetation and from the termite mound warms the eggs. All female crocodilians guard their nests, scaring away predators such as large lizards, birds and mammals. The eggs take 60 to 100 days to develop, depending on the species and the temperature of the nest. When baby crocodilians are ready to hatch, they call to their mothers, who scrape away nesting material to release their young. The mother and her young often stay together for several weeks or more until the young can fend for themselves.

LIFEGUARD
A female crocodile guards her nest covered with warm, rotting plant material for up to 100 days. During this time she does not leave the nest and will attack any intruder that comes too close.

BODYGUARD
Newly hatched crocodilians are eaten by many predators, from fish to birds (sometimes even other crocodilians). They stay close to their mother after they hatch, sometimes resting on her back, where no predator would dare to attack.

DID YOU KNOW?
Most female crocodilians continue to guard their own hatchlings for several weeks or months. But any adult crocodilian will answer a call of distress from a young crocodilian—even one that is five years old.

A SAFE PLACE
An alligator's jaws can be lethal, but this hatchling sits safely in its mother's mouth. It is being carried to a quiet pond, where the female alligator will protect it from predators.

Alligators and Caimans

Alligators and caimans are closely related, although they look quite different. The two species of alligator have broad snouts and large, rounded teeth. The American alligator grows to 20 ft (6 m) and lives in swamps and rivers in the southeastern part of North America. It eats fish, amphibians, reptiles, birds and mammals. Female American alligators occasionally attack humans, but usually only when they are protecting their nests. The 7 ft (2 m) Chinese alligator is found only around the Yangtze River in China. It eats snails, shellfish, insects and rats. All five species of caiman live in Central and South America. The black caiman, the largest species, grows to 20 ft (6 m) and lives in the flooded forests around the Amazon and Orinoco rivers. The smaller caimans have sharp, narrow teeth because they eat small prey, including snails, insects and frogs. They have strong bones in the scutes on their bellies and backs to protect them against predators.

LIVING IN DAMS
The common caiman is widespread in South America and is also found in Mexico. It grows to 10 ft (3 m), and often lives in cattle ponds and dams, where it mainly eats snails and fish.

REPTILIAN ARMOUR
Schneider's dwarf caiman, is hunted by anacondas and jaguars. Its skin contains many small bones, called osteoderms, which help protect it from predators. Even its eyelids are protected by bony plates.

SUBMARINE HUNTER
As an alligator approaches prey, it submerges and swims beneath the surface until it is close enough to attack. It moves so quietly and smoothly that the vegetation on top of the water is not even disturbed.

DEEP FREEZE
Chinese and American alligators can survive freezing winters in shallow pools. They keep their noses above water so that breathing holes form when the surface of the water freezes.

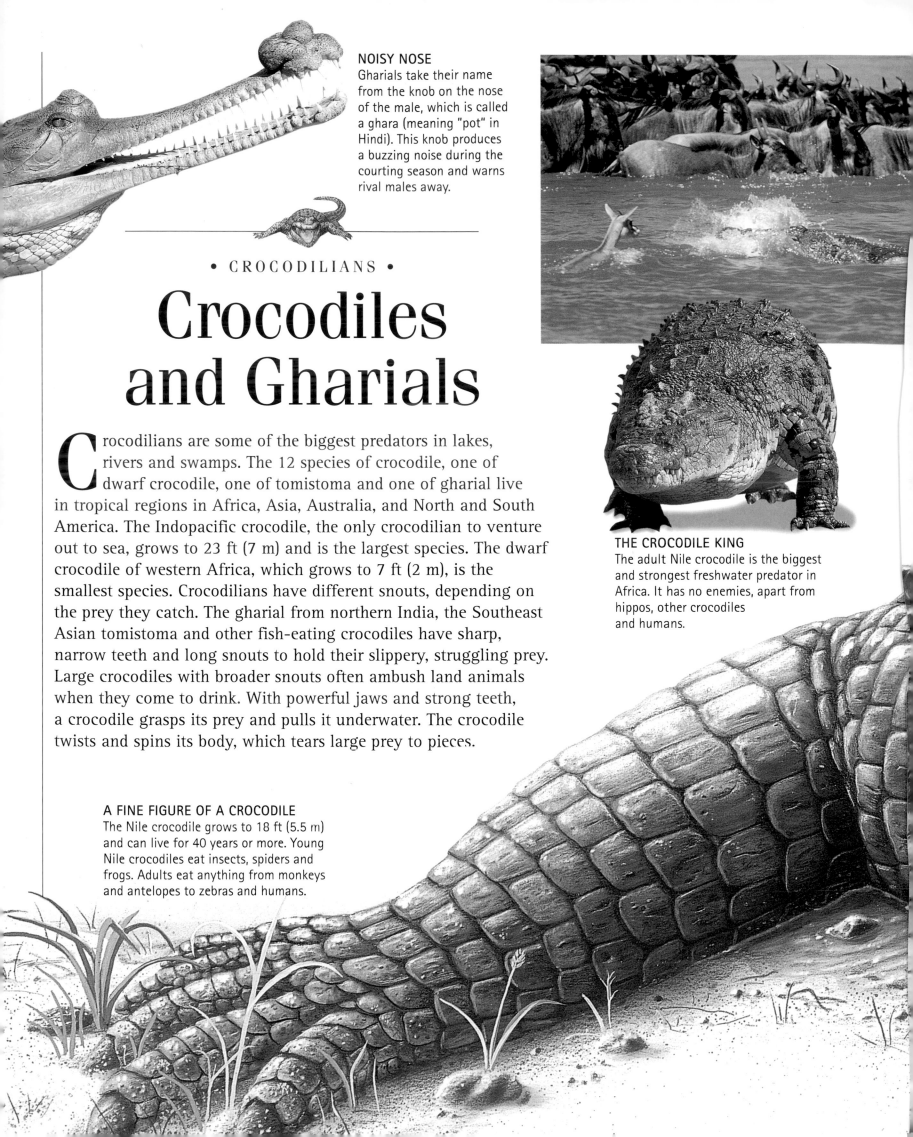

• CROCODILIANS •

Crocodiles and Gharials

Crocodilians are some of the biggest predators in lakes, rivers and swamps. The 12 species of crocodile, one of dwarf crocodile, one of tomistoma and one of gharial live in tropical regions in Africa, Asia, Australia, and North and South America. The Indopacific crocodile, the only crocodilian to venture out to sea, grows to 23 ft (7 m) and is the largest species. The dwarf crocodile of western Africa, which grows to 7 ft (2 m), is the smallest species. Crocodilians have different snouts, depending on the prey they catch. The gharial from northern India, the Southeast Asian tomistoma and other fish-eating crocodiles have sharp, narrow teeth and long snouts to hold their slippery, struggling prey. Large crocodiles with broader snouts often ambush land animals when they come to drink. With powerful jaws and strong teeth, a crocodile grasps its prey and pulls it underwater. The crocodile twists and spins its body, which tears large prey to pieces.

THE CROCODILE KING
The adult Nile crocodile is the biggest and strongest freshwater predator in Africa. It has no enemies, apart from hippos, other crocodiles and humans.

A FINE FIGURE OF A CROCODILE
The Nile crocodile grows to 18 ft (5.5 m) and can live for 40 years or more. Young Nile crocodiles eat insects, spiders and frogs. Adults eat anything from monkeys and antelopes to zebras and humans.

WILDEBEEST ATTACK
Large numbers of Nile crocodiles gather to attack herds of wildebeest as they cross rivers on their annual migration. Although they usually hunt alone, crocodiles do not compete with each other when there is plenty of food.

Protected back
A crocodile has small bones called osteoderms in the scutes on its back. These protect the crocodile from the bite of a predator or another crocodile.

MALE OR FEMALE?
A newborn male Nile crocodile crawls from its egg. The sex of a crocodilian is determined by the temperature inside the mother's nest. In the American alligator, for example, temperatures of 82°–86°F (28°–30°C) produce females; temperatures of 90°–93°F (32°–34°C) produce males. Temperatures in-between produce a mixture of males and females.

AGAINST THE ODDS
Female crocodilians care for their eggs and newly hatched young, but only a small number of hatchlings survive to become adults. Eggs can be crushed by a careless or inexperienced female, or dug up by large lizards, birds or mammals, such as mongooses. Hatchlings are eaten by water birds (below), hawks and eagles, fish and turtles—even larger crocodilians.

The Tuatara

The tuatara has changed little in 240 million years. It is often referred to as a "living fossil." Found only on a few small islands off the coast of New Zealand, tuataras are the oldest living relatives of today's snakes and lizards. The gray, olive or reddish tuatara looks a little like an iguana, but it is not a lizard at all. The two species of tuatara are the only living members of a group of small- to medium-sized reptiles called Rhynchocephalia, or "beak-heads." Rhynchocephalians lived in most parts of the world while the dinosaurs were alive. But by 60 million years ago, they were extinct everywhere except New Zealand, which had become isolated from other landmasses. When the Maoris of New Zealand first saw this unusual reptile, they called it "tuatara," which means "lightning back" and refers to the crest of large spikes on the male's back. Tuataras live in burrows. They eat earthworms, snails and insects, and hunt small lizards and hatchling birds. They crush and cut prey with their sharp, triangular teeth. Unlike the teeth of lizards, tuataras' teeth are permanently fused to the jaw.

SLOWLY DISAPPEARING?
Tuataras could once be found throughout the two main islands of New Zealand, but now they are restricted to 30 small islands off the northern coast of the North Island.

SIMILAR BUT NOT THE SAME
Tuataras may look like lizards, but they are very different. Tuataras, for example, have an extra bone in the skull. Lizards have two penises, but tuataras have none. A male and female tuatara mate by touching cloacae.

NIGHT BEAT
Tuataras hunt insects and other prey at night. They spend the day sleeping in their burrows or basking in the sunshine at their burrow entrances.

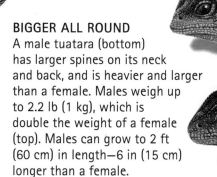

BIGGER ALL ROUND
A male tuatara (bottom) has larger spines on its neck and back, and is heavier and larger than a female. Males weigh up to 2.2 lb (1 kg), which is double the weight of a female (top). Males can grow to 2 ft (60 cm) in length—6 in (15 cm) longer than a female.

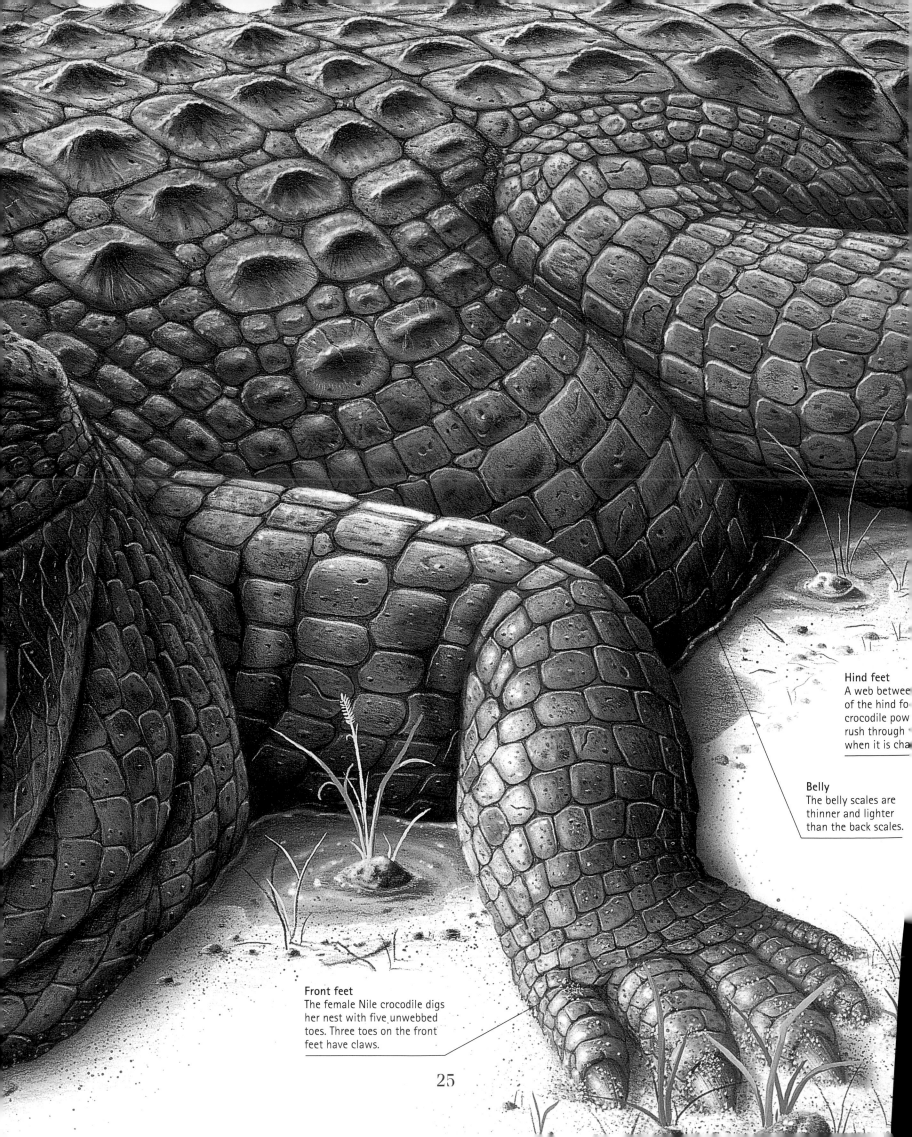

Hind feet
A web betwee
of the hind fo
crocodile pow
rush through
when it is cha

Belly
The belly scales are
thinner and lighter
than the back scales.

Front feet
The female Nile crocodile digs
her nest with five unwebbed
toes. Three toes on the front
feet have claws.

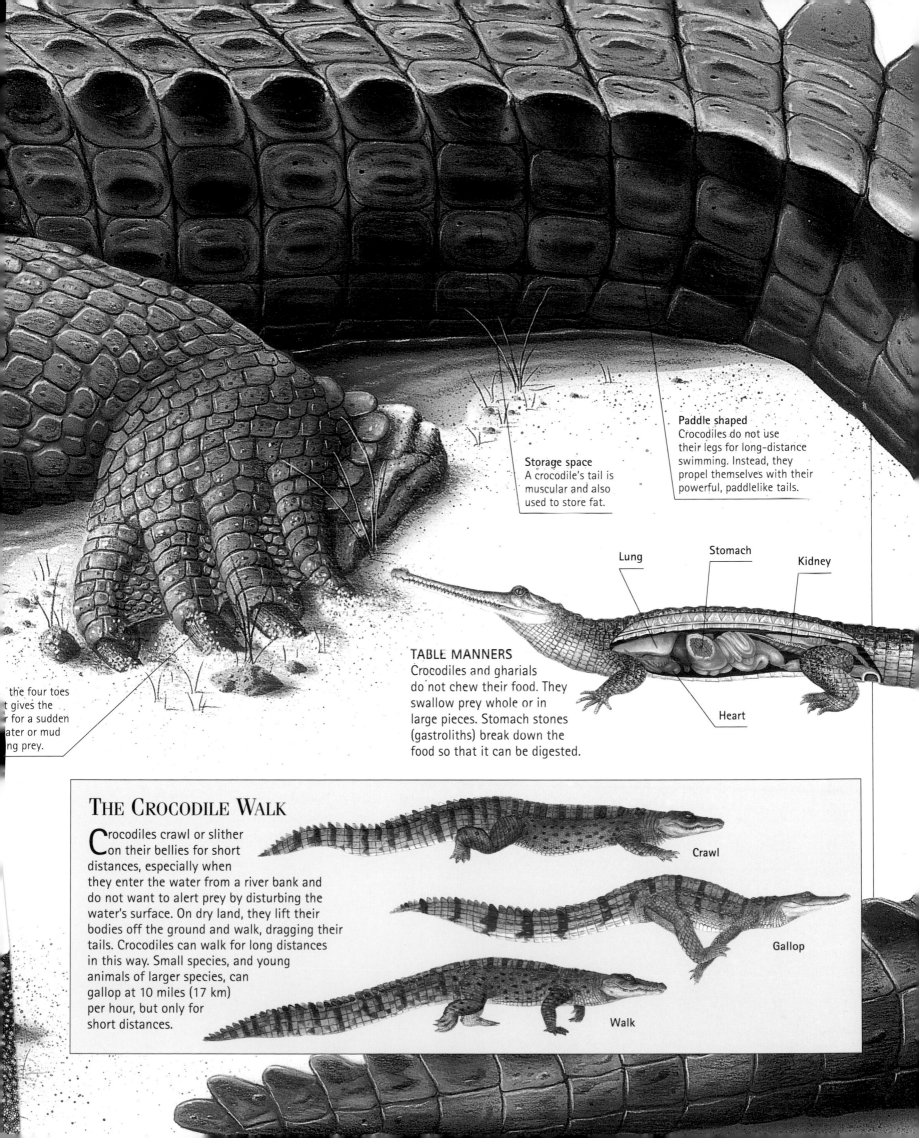

Storage space
A crocodile's tail is muscular and also used to store fat.

Paddle shaped
Crocodiles do not use their legs for long-distance swimming. Instead, they propel themselves with their powerful, paddlelike tails.

Lung   Stomach   Kidney

TABLE MANNERS
Crocodiles and gharials do not chew their food. They swallow prey whole or in large pieces. Stomach stones (gastroliths) break down the food so that it can be digested.

Heart

the four toes
t gives the
r for a sudden
ater or mud
ng prey.

THE CROCODILE WALK

Crocodiles crawl or slither on their bellies for short distances, especially when they enter the water from a river bank and do not want to alert prey by disturbing the water's surface. On dry land, they lift their bodies off the ground and walk, dragging their tails. Crocodiles can walk for long distances in this way. Small species, and young animals of larger species, can gallop at 10 miles (17 km) per hour, but only for short distances.

Crawl

Gallop

Walk

BELLOWING BEASTS

Crocodilians make more noise than any other reptiles, but they can also communicate without sound. American alligators tell other alligators where they are by a kind of silent purring that sends vibrations through the water (top). They end the silence with a loud bellow. During the breeding season, male crocodiles roar loudly, or lift their snouts out of the water and open their mouths to warn off other males (left).

JUMP SHOT

American alligators often hunt in water-bird colonies, where they eat fish that gather to feed on the birds' droppings. Occasionally, one will leap from the water to catch a young bird such as this egret chick, which has fallen from its nest.

Eighty million years ago, New Zealand became separated from other landmasses. While rhynchocephalians in other parts of the world died out, tuataras in New Zealand survived. Apart from birds, no large predators reached New Zealand until humans arrived a few thousand years ago. But humans brought with them dogs and Polynesian rats, and these animals began to eat tuatara eggs and hatchlings. Today, tuataras can be found only on islands without rats.

DINNER TIME
Tuataras are not fast runners. They sit still and wait for prey to come close enough so they can lunge at it. This tuatara has spotted a large weta, or New Zealand cricket, and is waiting for a chance to pounce.

DID YOU KNOW?
Tuataras in the south live in a much colder environment and grow more slowly than tuataras in the north. No-one knows exactly how long tuataras live, but it may be for up to 120 years.

Discover more in Early Reptiles

Looking at Lizards

BITE-SIZED
This baby Madagascan chameleon will grow to 3½ in (9 cm). But the smallest lizard, the Virgin Islands gecko, is only 1½ in (3.5 cm) when fully grown.

FLYING LEAP
The flying gecko of Southeast Asia has flaps of skin along its sides, and glides from tree to tree to escape predators.

There are approximately 3,750 species of lizard in the world. They come in all shapes and sizes, from the tiny gecko to the 10-ft (3-m) long Komodo dragon. Some are short and flat; others are legless and snakelike. Some lizards are brightly colored, while others are dull and blend into the background. Although most lizards are tropical, they are also found in cold climates and from sea level to mountains as high as 16,400 ft (5,000 m). Some Asian and North American skinks hibernate over winter in burrows beneath the snow, emerging in spring to feed on insects attracted to spring flowers. Most lizards are predators, and eat everything from ants and insects to other lizards and animals as large as goats. Lizards also play an important role in controlling insect pests. A house gecko, for example, can eat half its own weight in small insects in a single night. Many large lizards, such as skinks and iguanas, eat mainly plants and fruit. The marine iguanas of the Galápagos Islands eat mostly seaweed.

ON THE LOOKOUT
With long legs and a strong body, monitor lizards are fast runners that usually live in deserts or grasslands. Monitors are found in Africa, Asia and Australia, and include the largest of the lizards, the Komodo dragon.

DID YOU KNOW?
The horned chameleon's eyes are mounted in turrets and can look in different directions at the same time. It can find prey with one eye and watch for predators with the other.

A wall lizard has the most common lizard shape—ideal for hunting and hiding.

The sail-tailed water dragon swims with its high, flattened tail.

A monitor has a long, flexible body for hunting over long distances.

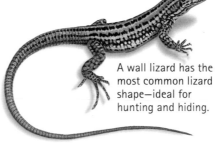

The legless lizard has a streamlined body for moving in narrow places.

The flat body of the desert short-horned lizard helps it hide from predators.

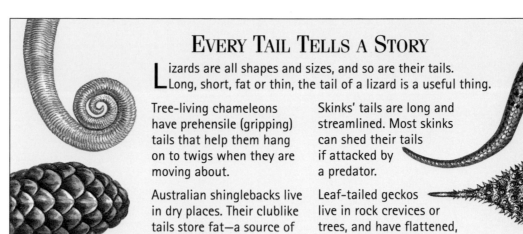

EVERY TAIL TELLS A STORY

Lizards are all shapes and sizes, and so are their tails. Long, short, fat or thin, the tail of a lizard is a useful thing.

Tree-living chameleons have prehensile (gripping) tails that help them hang on to twigs when they are moving about.

Australian shinglebacks live in dry places. Their clublike tails store fat—a source of energy and water.

Skinks' tails are long and streamlined. Most skinks can shed their tails if attacked by a predator.

Leaf-tailed geckos live in rock crevices or trees, and have flattened, camouflaged tails.

A FINE FIGURE

Boyd's forest dragon, from northeastern Australia, is one of the largest dragon lizards in the world. It can puff out its dewlap (a flap of skin on its throat) to communicate with other forest dragons in its rainforest home.

Lizard Facts

Lizards can be found in almost every environment, from rainforests to baking deserts, but they have many features in common. All lizards, for example, have scaly skin. Daytime lizards have rough skins, while night-time lizards, such as geckos, have small, beadlike scales. Most burrowing lizards have smooth scales to help them push through the soil. Lizards have developed special features for their different habitats. Those that live above the ground have external ear openings and large eyes. Lizards that live beneath the ground have tiny eyes, and their external ear openings are covered by scaly skin. Most lizards have fleshy pink tongues, but monitor lizards have slender forked tongues, which they use to "taste" chemicals in the air. Some lizards have flashy blue tongues that they stick out to startle predators. Lizards eat mainly insects and other invertebrates, which they crush with their pointed teeth. Plant-eating lizards have flattened teeth for chopping their food, while lizards that eat snails have flat, rounded teeth for crushing shells.

A GOOD GRIP
A gecko's toe pad has thousands of fine hairlike projections. These cling to invisible rough spots and allow a gecko to walk on walls and upside down on ceilings.

A MOUTHFUL OF FOOD
Most lizards have pointed teeth that are all the same shape. This means that lizards cannot cut up or chew their food. Instead, they crush prey with their teeth and then swallow it whole.

DID YOU KNOW?

A legless lizard and a snake may seem similar, but look at them closely. Most legless lizards have small ear openings behind the eyes, but snakes have no ears at all. Legless lizards also have pointed tongues while snakes have forked tongues.

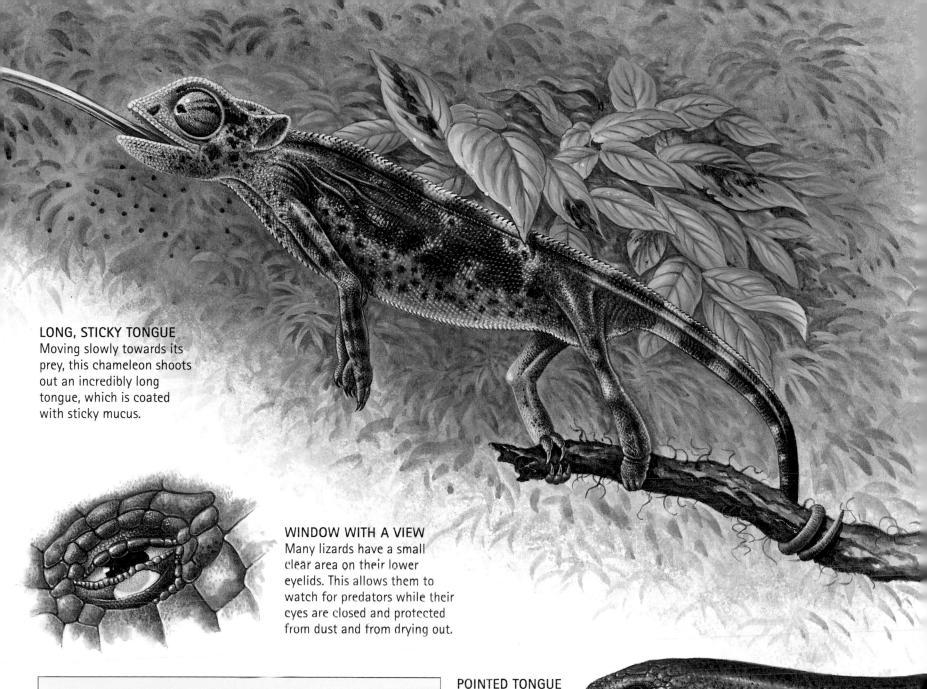

LONG, STICKY TONGUE
Moving slowly towards its prey, this chameleon shoots out an incredibly long tongue, which is coated with sticky mucus.

WINDOW WITH A VIEW
Many lizards have a small clear area on their lower eyelids. This allows them to watch for predators while their eyes are closed and protected from dust and from drying out.

DISAPPEARING LEGS

Most lizards have four well-developed legs, but some lizards have reduced limbs or no limbs at all. These lizards usually burrow, or live in habitats where limbs would be of little use, such as areas with many narrow crevices. Lizards lost their limbs or developed reduced limbs over thousands of years. The front limbs of these lizards usually changed before the back limbs. The bones either became smaller overall or they were lost altogether. When this happened, the toes were the first bones to disappear (as shown).

No toes

Reduced toes

Well-developed toes

POINTED TONGUE
A European slow worm uses its pointed tongue to catch prey.

FLASHY TONGUE
A shingleback lizard startles prey with its flattened tongue.

FORKED TONGUE
A goanna detects prey with its forked tongue.

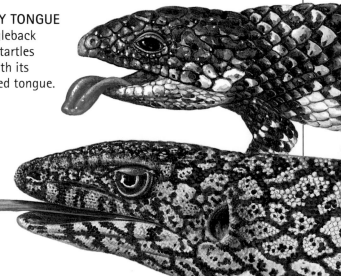

The Next Generation

Most lizards lay eggs. Some geckos and skinks lay only one, while larger lizards may lay as many as forty. A few lizards guard their eggs against predators, but most simply lay their eggs, cover them with soil or leaves, and leave them. Other lizards give birth to fully formed ("live") young. The eggs are protected inside the female bodies, and the developing young are nourished by yolk in the same way as young that grow in eggs outside the body. The female European common lizard lays eggs in warm climates, but in cool mountain climates where the temperature may not be high enough for eggs to develop properly, the female gives birth to live young. Lizards are able to look after themselves as soon as they hatch, but dangers await the next generation. There are many creatures, such as spiders, insects, lizards, snakes, birds and mammals, waiting to eat them. Very few young lizards survive to breed.

HOUSE GUESTS
Some species of goanna (Australian monitors) keep their eggs warm and safe by laying them in termite mounds. The female has to scrape away the hard soil to help her hatchlings escape.

DID YOU KNOW?
Geckos lay hard-shelled eggs that often stick to tree bark or leaves. These tough eggs can be carried far out to sea, on a large branch or trunk broken off in a storm. Geckos are found on many islands that other lizards have not reached.

THE RIGHT TIME
The female collared lizard can store eggs in her body until laying conditions are right; for example, there must be enough moisture in the ground to keep the eggs from drying out.

BREAK-OUT
A collared lizard cuts its way out of the egg with an "egg tooth"—a special tooth on the tip of its upper lip—which drops off soon after hatching. It fends for itself as soon as it is born.

SINGLE PARENTS
Some chameleons, dragon lizards, night lizards, whiptail lizards (below), wall lizards and geckos reproduce without males. The eggs of these lizards do not need to be fertilized by males. These all-female lizards increase in number faster than those that have male and female parents.

A SMALL LITTER
Many skinks give birth to live young rather than laying eggs. The Australian shingleback usually gives birth to two live young— a small litter for a lizard.

A LARGE LITTER
The Australian blue-tongue skink gives birth to several lizards. These young, however, are smaller than lizards born in a small litter.

Discover more in Temperature Control

Temperature Control

Lizards and other reptiles regulate their body temperature by their behavior. To warm up, they move into the sun or onto a warm surface and expose as much of their body as they can to the heat. To cool down, they expose as little of their body as possible to the heat, or they move into the shade or a crevice. Many desert and tropical lizards can be active at night because the night-time temperatures in these environments are mild. In extremely cold climates, lizards spend the winter in a deep burrow or crevice. Birds and mammals are called warm-blooded because they regulate their body temperature internally and are always warm. Warm-blooded animals must constantly use energy to stay warm. Reptiles, however, are cold-blooded animals. They cool down when they are not warmed by outside heat, and use a lot of energy only when they are warm and active.

COOL CHANGE
In hot climates, lizards hide in crevices or burrows during the hottest part of the day. These cool places often trap a little water, and the sheltered lizard can breathe moist air, which also helps to keep it cool.

Energetic
With its body warmed, a sand lizard has energy for hunting, mating and defending its territory.

SHADES OF THE DAY
In the morning and late afternoon, the skin of rhinoceros iguanas is dark, to absorb the heat of the sun. During the hottest part of the day, their skins are lighter. This helps them to reflect as much heat as possible.

A MIDDAY BURROWER
This common barking gecko is nocturnal and emerges to hunt in the early evening.

Resting
A sand lizard basks in the sun to warm its body and get energy for a day of activity.

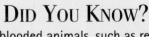

DID YOU KNOW?
Cold-blooded animals, such as reptiles, are able to survive extreme conditions such as drought and cold weather. Their heart rate slows down, they breathe more slowly, and their digestive systems stop working.

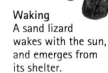

Waking
A sand lizard wakes with the sun, and emerges from its shelter.

36

Hiding out
A sand lizard seeks shelter during the warmest part of the day to avoid overheating.

NIGHT LIFE

Some lizards, such as geckos, are active at night. They emerge shortly after dark and take advantage of the still-warm ground to hunt insects. Nocturnal lizards need to be able to see in the dark. They have big eyes and their pupils—the transparent "holes" that let light into the eyes—are large, vertical slits. At night, these open wide to let in as much light as possible.

Energetic
In the early afternoon, a sand lizard resumes its activities.

A DAY IN THE LIFE OF A LIZARD

Like most land reptiles that are out in daylight, a sand lizard moves around and rests during the day. The temperature and the surroundings influence the way the sand lizard spends its day.

SUN BATHING

Even if clouds hide the sun in the afternoon, lizards can soak up heat (energy for afternoon activities) by pressing against rocks that have been warmed earlier in the day.

Resting
Late afternoon is the time to bask and digest the day's meal of insects.

End of the day
As the sun sinks, a sand lizard begins to move into its retreat.

Ready for sleep
A sand lizard curls up to stay as protected as possible through the night.

37

VENOMOUS MONSTER
The 18 in (45 cm) Gila monster of North America is one of the world's two venomous lizards, though its bite is rarely fatal to humans. The Gila monster stores fat in its thick tail, and uses this supply of energy to survive without food for several months.

"HOT-SPOT" TACTICS
A zebra-tailed lizard mesmerizes its predator with the black-and-white pattern under its tail. Then it races off, leaving the predator staring fixedly at the spot where the waving tail once was.

PRICKLY CREATURE
The thorny devil of central Australia may look fearsome, but it is actually a harmless eater of ants. It is very well adapted to desert life: for example, the pattern of scales on its body channels rainwater to its mouth.

• A LIZARD'S LIFE •

Living in Dry Places

Lizards that live in dry or arid places have to cope with high temperatures and little water. They deal with scorching temperatures in different ways. Many species, for example, are nocturnal. They hunt in the early evening for several hours when the ground is still warm. Daytime species burrow into cool sand or hide in crevices and beneath rocks during the hottest part of the day. Some raise themselves on their toes to keep away from hot sand, or they run to shelter. Finding water is a more serious problem. Most desert lizards, such as the one above, get most of the water they need from food. Their bodies convert the prey they eat into fat, which they store in their tails. The fat is then converted into energy, a process that produces water for the body. All lizards produce droppings that are almost dry, which minimizes the precious water they lose from their bodies.

SMOOTH MOVES
Desert-burrowing lizards are known as "sand swimmers" or "sand fish," because they seem to be able to swim through loose sand. Sand swimmers use their wedge-shaped snouts to "dive" beneath the surface of the sand to escape predators.

FOOT SPECIALISTS

Many sand-dwelling lizards have webbed feet or fringed toes to help them grip shifting sand. A desert gecko's foot (right) is webbed to help it dig burrows and to move across sand dunes to look for food or to escape from predators. The toes of the fringe-toed lizard (below) have featherlike scales to grip sand when the lizard needs to chase prey or run from predators. The fringes on its toes may also help this lizard to cool its feet so that it does not become too hot.

TOO HOT TO HANDLE
This desert fringe-toed lizard lifts one front leg and the opposite back leg, then balances on its other legs for a few moments to cool its feet. Some dragon lizards of dry inland Australia avoid hot surfaces by raising their hind toes.

Discover more in Land Tortoises

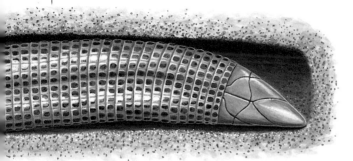

PREY UNDERGROUND
Worm lizards can dig quickly to reach insect prey, which they detect from underground vibrations. They also use their sharp teeth and powerful jaws to crush any invertebrates they meet while they are digging their tunnels.

DIGGING FROM SIDE TO SIDE
Keel-snouted worm lizards use their wedge-shaped snouts to scrape soil from the front of the tunnel. They compress the soil into the side of the tunnel with their heads as they move forward.

DIGGING UP AND DOWN
The shovel-snouted worm lizard grows to 4–30 in (10–75 cm) long. It uses its broad, hard head to push soil upwards and compacts it into the top of the tunnel. Body scales arranged like tiles help to keep dirt from building up on its body.

Underground Life

Amphisbaenians (worm lizards) are some of the strangest lizards in the world. All 140 species of amphisbaenian ("am-fizz-BEEN-ee-an") spend most of their lives underground, beneath leaf-litter in the forests of the warmer parts of Africa, Southeast Asia, Europe and the United States. There are four families of worm lizards, and three of these have no legs at all. Mexican worm lizards, however, have two strong front legs. Worm lizards have cylinder-shaped bodies and burrow through tunnels with their hard, strong heads. Most lizards move by using their legs, but worm lizards move like snakes in confined spaces: they inch their way through tunnels in a straight line. All worm lizards have simplified eyes that are covered by clear skin. They crush insects and other invertebrates with their sharp teeth and strong jaws. They have no external ear openings (these would be clogged by dirt), but they can sense prey and predators through vibrations in the soil. Most species lay eggs, but a few worm lizards give birth to live young.

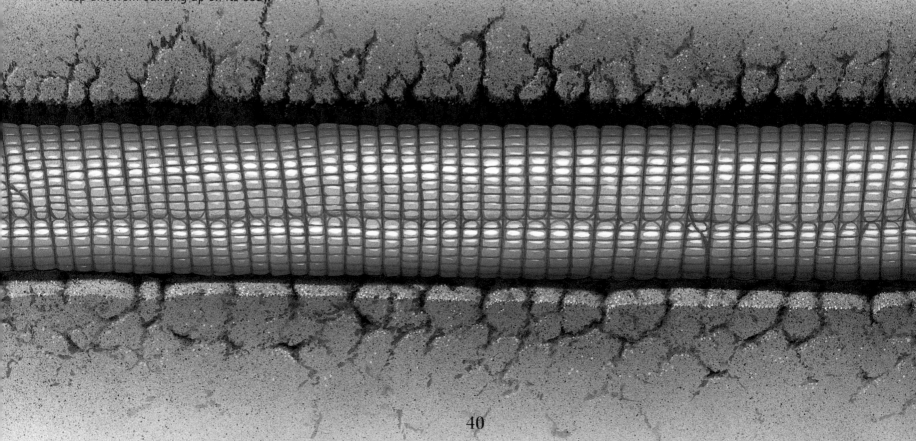

HEADS AND TAILS
The exposed tail of a burrowing worm lizard is protected from predators because it is very hard. The worm has large head scales to strengthen its head for digging.

DIGGING TOOLS
The Mexican worm lizard has strong front legs that are flattened like paddles to help it move above ground. When it begins digging a tunnel, the lizard swings its legs forward and sweeps soil back past its head.

DIFFERENT HEADS

Round-headed

Keel-headed

Shovel-headed

Chisel-headed

Most worm lizards burrow with their heads. The way different groups of worm lizards burrow is reflected in the different shapes of their heads. Round-headed species push forward into the earth and turn the head in any direction to make the burrow. Keel-headed species push the head forward and then to the side. Shovel-headed species push forward and then push the head up. Chisel-headed species rotate the head in one direction and then in the other.

THE TAIL END
This worm lizard looks as if it has two heads, but one end is in fact its tail. Like many other lizards, worm lizards can shed their tails if they are grabbed by a predator.

Invisible eye
The worm lizard's eye is very simple and sometimes not even visible. It can barely see movement, and can only distinguish between light and dark.

Hard snout
A worm lizard has a large reinforced scale as a snout. This helps it to force its way through the soil.

Tucked-in mouth
The worm lizard's mouth is tucked beneath the snout, so dirt cannot get into it when the worm is burrowing.

Discover more in Looking at Lizards

Defense and Escape

Lizards have many enemies. Spiders, scorpions, other lizards, snakes, birds and mammals all prey on them. The Gila monster and the Mexican beaded lizard are the only venomous lizards; other species of lizard have special tactics to defend themselves or to escape from an attacker. Most lizards are well camouflaged and may keep absolutely still until a predator passes by. Chameleons can change their color to blend in with their background, and also stay completely still when a tree snake or other predator approaches. Some lizards surprise or distract a predator to give themselves a chance to escape. The Australian frilled lizard opens its frill suddenly. Other lizards extend their neck or throat crest, hiss, or swallow air to look bigger than an attacker (or too big to swallow). Some even stick out their colored tongues! Many lizards have an unusual method of escape. If grabbed by the tail, they leave it behind. A wriggling tail helps to distract an attacker. Running away, out of a predator's reach, is also a good defense. Some lizards have sharp spines that can injure a predator's mouth, or slippery scales that make them hard to grip.

BOO!
Some lizards try to frighten attackers by pretending to be bigger than they really are. The Australian frilled lizard startles a predator by opening its mouth, hissing loudly and flourishing the frill behind its neck.

ON GUARD!
The armadillo girdle-tailed lizard curls itself into a ball when it is threatened and protects its soft belly with a prickly fence.

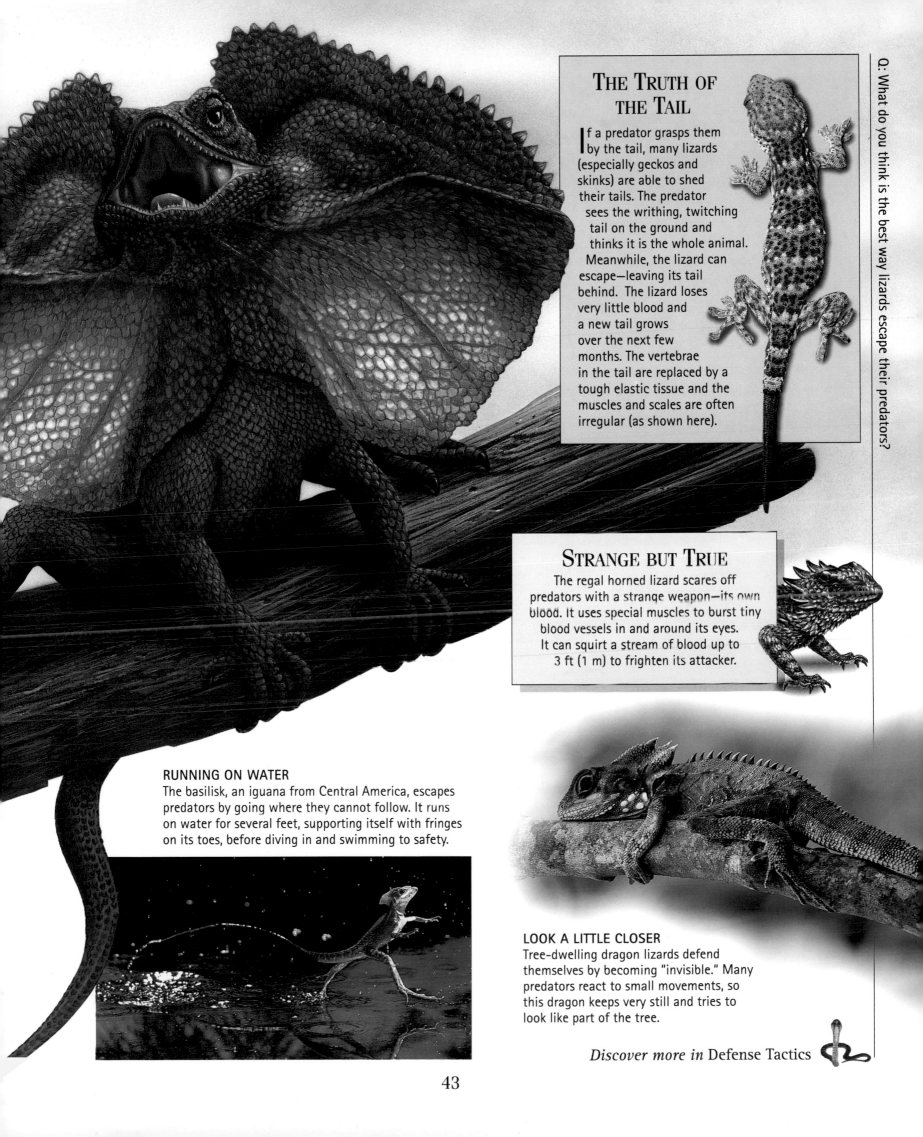

Q: What do you think is the best way lizards escape their predators?

THE TRUTH OF THE TAIL

If a predator grasps them by the tail, many lizards (especially geckos and skinks) are able to shed their tails. The predator sees the writhing, twitching tail on the ground and thinks it is the whole animal. Meanwhile, the lizard can escape—leaving its tail behind. The lizard loses very little blood and a new tail grows over the next few months. The vertebrae in the tail are replaced by a tough elastic tissue and the muscles and scales are often irregular (as shown here).

STRANGE BUT TRUE

The regal horned lizard scares off predators with a strange weapon—its own blood. It uses special muscles to burst tiny blood vessels in and around its eyes. It can squirt a stream of blood up to 3 ft (1 m) to frighten its attacker.

RUNNING ON WATER

The basilisk, an iguana from Central America, escapes predators by going where they cannot follow. It runs on water for several feet, supporting itself with fringes on its toes, before diving in and swimming to safety.

LOOK A LITTLE CLOSER

Tree-dwelling dragon lizards defend themselves by becoming "invisible." Many predators react to small movements, so this dragon keeps very still and tries to look like part of the tree.

Discover more in Defense Tactics

43

Keeping in Touch

PUSHING UP
Collared lizards communicate with each other by bobbing their heads up and down. If another lizard enters their territory, they threaten the invader by performing "push-ups" that make them look bigger.

Most lizards live alone. They come in contact with other members of their species only for courtship and mating, and to fight over living areas. Lizards communicate in a number of ways such as raising crests, extending or curling dewlaps, waving a front limb or lashing the tail, or changing color. Iguanas and dragon lizards wave one leg in the air, bob their heads or move their bodies up and down to let other lizards know they are ready to mate, or to warn invaders to leave their territories. Male chameleons change color to threaten rivals, while other male lizards change color to let females know they are ready to mate (some female lizards change color after they have laid their eggs to let males know they are not interested in mating).

Most geckos are active at night when color and movement are not easy to see, so some species keep in touch by calling to each other. Barking or chirping sounds, for example, warn other geckos to keep away.

RED IN THE FACE
Male chameleons can change their dull camouflage colors to bright colors to warn other males away from their territories. This species changes color from a calm green to a threatening red to intimidate a rival.

MATING SIGNALS
Male and female marine iguanas of the Galápagos Islands are usually a grayish-black color. In the breeding season, the spiny crests and front limbs of the males turn green and the sides of their bodies become rusty red. Females know the males are ready to mate.

Q: How do female marine iguanas know when males are ready to mate?

TOO BIG A MOUTHFUL
Bearded dragon lizards open their brightly colored mouths to surprise predators. They also expand their throats to make themselves look too big for a predator to eat, or too big for a rival dragon to fight.

DANGER SIGNALS
Male anole lizards have a brightly colored dewlap that they expand in a sudden flash of color to warn other males or to attract females.

WORSE THAN THEIR BITE
In Southeast Asia, barking house geckos (called "dup-dups" in Malaysia because of the sound they make) keep in touch with their mates or warn other geckos away from their hunting territories with chirping sounds or sharp barks.

CHEMICAL COMMUNICATION
Lizards need to figure out if another lizard is a potential mate or a rival. One way they do this is through pheromones, special chemicals produced by glands in the skin. Pheromones are detected by the nose and by a structure in the roof of the mouth called Jacobson's organ. When the lizard flicks out its tongue (below), it picks up important chemical scents and pheromones from the ground or the air. The tongue then carries these molecules back to the roof of the mouth.

Sizing up Snakes

There are almost 2,400 species of snake. From the 8-in (20-cm) long thread snake to the giant anaconda, which can reach 36 ft (11 m) and weigh 440 lb (200 kg), snakes have many different colors, patterns and ways of killing their prey. Snakes eat everything from ants, eggs, snails and slugs to animals as big as caimans and goats. Snakes can swallow large prey because they have elastic connections between some of the bones in their skulls, especially those between the skull and the lower jaws. Some snakes are very venomous: a single drop of venom from the Australian small-scaled snake can kill thousands of mice. Certain kinds of cobra spit venom to blind their predators, while non-venomous pythons wrap themselves around their prey, tightening their grip to overcome it. Some snakes have smooth skin, while the skin of others is very rough. Filesnakes use their sandpaper-like skin to hold their slippery prey of fish.

ENTWINED IN VINES
The vine snake of Central and South America grows to 7 ft (2 m), but its body is no more than ½ in (1.3 cm) round. Its green colors blend in with leaves, and its slender body enables it to move rapidly across branches in search of prey such as small birds in nests.

PATTERN WITH A PURPOSE
Many snakes, especially venomous ones, are brightly colored to warn predators that they are very dangerous. Some harmless species, such as this milk snake, copy the colors of venomous snakes for the same effect.

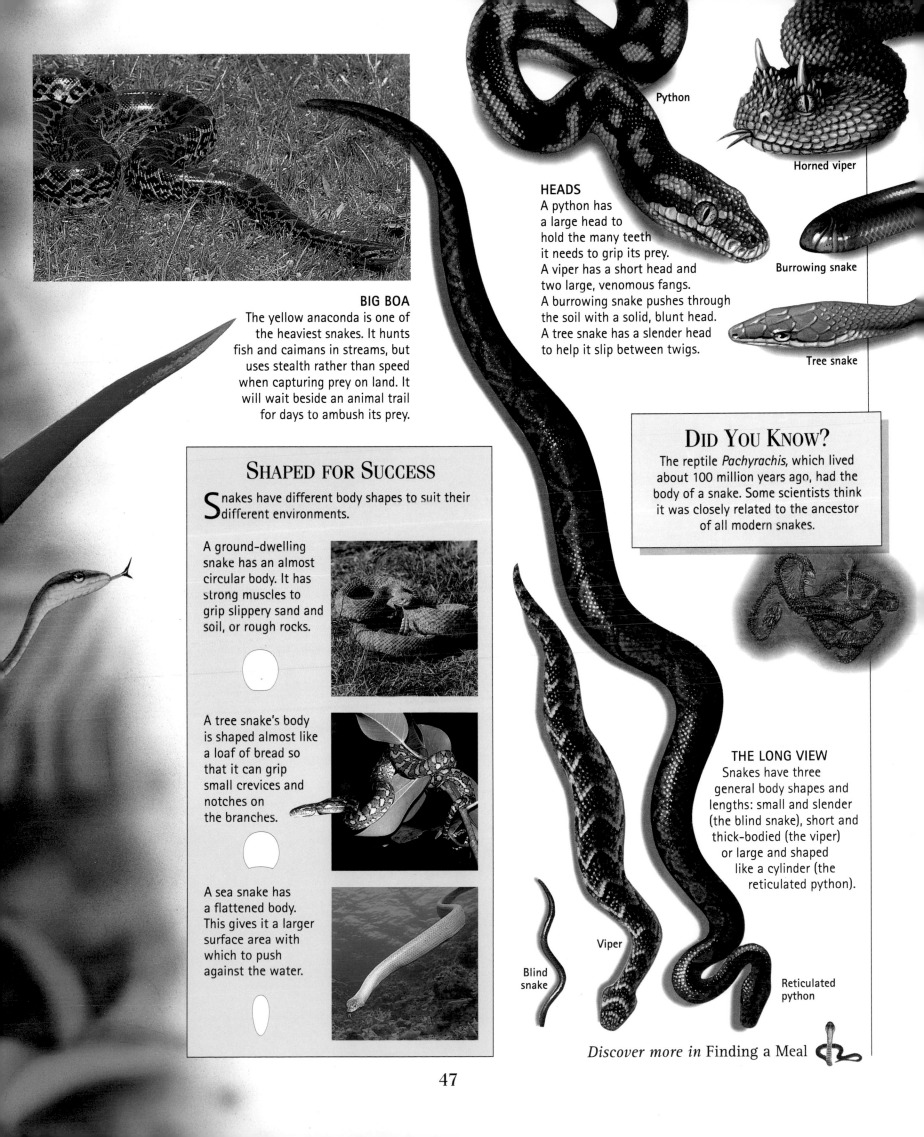

BIG BOA

The yellow anaconda is one of the heaviest snakes. It hunts fish and caimans in streams, but uses stealth rather than speed when capturing prey on land. It will wait beside an animal trail for days to ambush its prey.

HEADS

A python has a large head to hold the many teeth it needs to grip its prey. A viper has a short head and two large, venomous fangs. A burrowing snake pushes through the soil with a solid, blunt head. A tree snake has a slender head to help it slip between twigs.

Python

Horned viper

Burrowing snake

Tree snake

SHAPED FOR SUCCESS

Snakes have different body shapes to suit their different environments.

A ground-dwelling snake has an almost circular body. It has strong muscles to grip slippery sand and soil, or rough rocks.

A tree snake's body is shaped almost like a loaf of bread so that it can grip small crevices and notches on the branches.

A sea snake has a flattened body. This gives it a larger surface area with which to push against the water.

DID YOU KNOW?

The reptile *Pachyrachis,* which lived about 100 million years ago, had the body of a snake. Some scientists think it was closely related to the ancestor of all modern snakes.

THE LONG VIEW

Snakes have three general body shapes and lengths: small and slender (the blind snake), short and thick-bodied (the viper) or large and shaped like a cylinder (the reticulated python).

Blind snake

Viper

Reticulated python

Discover more in Finding a Meal

Snake Specifications

As snakes evolved from lizards, they became long and slender, and lost their limbs. Some of their internal organs, such as the liver and the lungs, also became long and thin. Others, such as the kidneys and reproductive organs, were rearranged one behind the other in the body. In many snakes the left lung even disappeared! Unlike animals with limbs, snakes can escape from predators or hunt prey by squeezing into narrow spaces. Snakes have sharp, pointed teeth and, in some cases, venom to help them kill prey. With their long, supple bodies, snakes can form tight coils to strangle their prey, wrap around their eggs to keep them warm, or curl into a ball to deter predators. Snakes live in many environments and their scales can be rough or smooth. As a snake grows, it sheds its scaly skin and reveals a new skin underneath.

THE SCENT OF PREY

Most snakes are carnivores. They use their sensitive tongues to "taste" the air and pick up chemicals produced by prey. A newly hatched snake eats small animals such as frogs and lizards. As it grows bigger, its prey becomes larger.

SHEDDING

Snakes shed their skins when they grow too big for them. To loosen its skin, a snake rubs its nose against a hard surface. Then it wriggles free. The old skin (including the snake's clear eyelids) comes off inside-out.

DID YOU KNOW?

Some pythons and blind snakes have tiny leftovers of their hind limbs. These are visible as a pair of "spurs" on the sides of the body, close to the snake's tail. Male pythons use their spurs in combat and courtship.

CLOSE TO THE GROUND

Snakes have completely lost their limbs. They move by using the muscles attached to their ribs.

A USEFUL SCALE

Snake scales give us clues about how and where snakes live. Most snakes that live in wetlands and fresh water have keeled scales. These help to balance side-to-side movement and provide a larger surface area for heating and cooling. Snakes that burrow usually have smooth scales, as these make it easier for them to push through the soil. Many water and sea snakes have "granular" scales with a rough, grainy surface like sandpaper, which helps them to grip their slippery prey.

Keeled scales

Smooth scales

Granular scales

CONTACT LENS
Snakes do not have movable eyelids. Their eyes are covered by a special clear eyelid that protects the eye from damage. Nocturnal species often have vertical pupils, like the eyes of cats.

SMALL EYES
Nocturnal snakes are active at night. They have small eyes and do not rely heavily on sight to hunt. Instead, they use their tongues to detect their prey, or special heat-sensing organs to sense warm-blooded animals.

BIG EYES
Diurnal snakes, which are active in daylight, have large eyes because they rely mainly on sight to find their prey. However, these snakes also use their tongues to detect prey and predators.

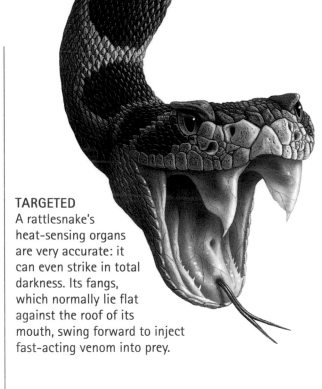

TARGETED
A rattlesnake's heat-sensing organs are very accurate: it can even strike in total darkness. Its fangs, which normally lie flat against the roof of its mouth, swing forward to inject fast-acting venom into prey.

EGG MEAL
The African egg-eating snake stretches its jaw to wrap its mouth around the egg.

CRUSHED
The eggshell is crushed by the ridges that project into the snake's throat from its backbone.

SHELL REJECTED
After swallowing the liquid contents of the egg, the snake regurgitates the crushed eggshell.

DID YOU KNOW?
Most snakes eat only one large prey at each meal. Burrowing snakes and blind snakes (shown), however, are unusual. Like lizards, they eat small prey, such as ant eggs, frequently.

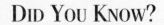

Finding a Meal

All snakes eat animals. Some will ambush, stalk or pursue their prey. Others eat "easy" prey, such as the eggs of birds and reptiles (including those of other snakes). A few snakes eat snails (which they pull out of their shells), worms and crabs. Many snakes, such as pythons and boa constrictors, kill their prey by constricting, or squeezing it. A python, for example, wraps itself around an animal. Whenever the animal breathes out, the python squeezes a little tighter, until the animal suffocates. More than half of all snakes kill their prey with venom, which is produced by highly evolved mouth glands and injected through hollow or grooved fangs. Rattlesnakes have small pits on the front of their faces; many pythons and some boas have pits in their lip scales. These pits contain heat sensors that can detect temperature differences of one thousandth of a degree. They tell the snake how far away its prey is, and even where the heart (the warmest part of the animal) is. This means the snake can strike its prey with deadly accuracy.

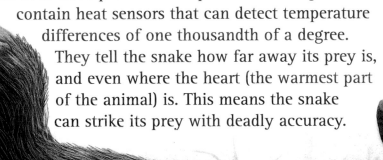

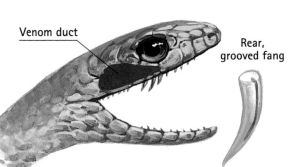

Venom duct

Rear, grooved fang

REAR FANGS
Rear-fanged snakes have fixed fangs, located towards the back of the mouth. Venom travels down grooves along the length of the fangs.

FIXED FRONT FANGS
Cobras and their relatives have hollow, fixed fangs in the front of the mouth.

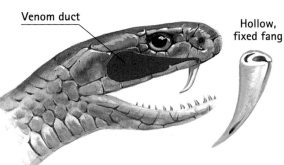

Venom duct

Hollow, fixed fang

DID YOU KNOW?
Australia has more venomous snakes than any other country, but only two or three Australians die each year from snakebite. However, thousands of people die from snakebite each year in rural India, where people often walk around barefoot.

Hollow, swinging fang

Venom duct

SWINGING FRONT FANGS
Vipers and rattlesnakes have large, hollow fangs that swing forward to the front of the mouth.

CHOOSE YOUR POISON
Snake venoms affect their prey in one of two different ways. The neurotoxic venoms of the cobras and their relatives act on the nerves to stop the heart and damage the lungs. The hemotoxic venoms of vipers and rattlesnakes destroy muscles. Snake venom probably evolved to help snakes capture prey, but they also use it to defend themselves. Most venomous snakes are highly resistant to their own venom.

SUDDEN DEATH
A rattlesnake's venom is not as powerful as that of the cobra and many of its relatives, but it injects a large amount through its long fangs. The venom acts quickly, paralyzing or killing prey, such as rodents.

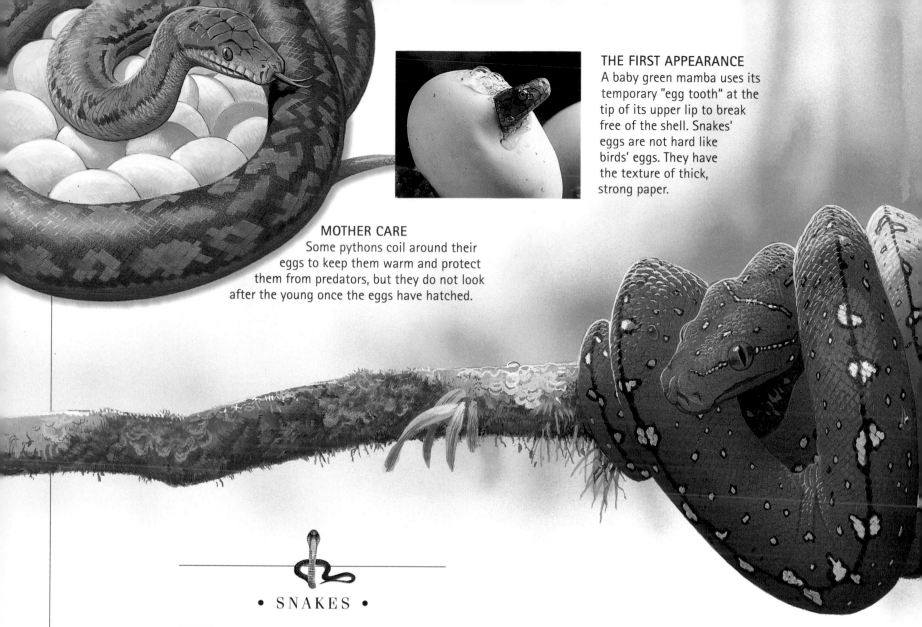

THE FIRST APPEARANCE
A baby green mamba uses its temporary "egg tooth" at the tip of its upper lip to break free of the shell. Snakes' eggs are not hard like birds' eggs. They have the texture of thick, strong paper.

MOTHER CARE
Some pythons coil around their eggs to keep them warm and protect them from predators, but they do not look after the young once the eggs have hatched.

• SNAKES •

Early Life

Each spring in mild climates, or just before the rainy season in the tropics, snakes begin to mate and reproduce. In most egg-laying species the female looks for a safe, warm and slightly moist place—such as a rotting log, or beneath a rock—to lay her eggs. Once she has laid the eggs, she covers them and leaves the eggs to develop and hatch on their own. A few species of snake, however, do stay with their eggs until they have hatched. Female pythons coil themselves around the eggs to keep them warm, and both male and female cobras guard their eggs. But once the young have hatched, pythons and cobras also leave them to look after themselves. Some snakes, such as most vipers and various water snakes, give birth to fully developed young. "Live-bearing" snakes tend to live in cool climates or watery habitats. Scientists believe this type of birth occurs in cool climates because the eggs would be generally warmer in the mother's body than in the soil. Snakes in wet environments give birth to live young because eggs could drown in water or become moldy in soil.

BRIEF ENCOUNTERS
Snakes are usually solitary animals and live by themselves. They come together briefly either to mate, or when two males fight to test their strength.

BRIGHT CAMOUFLAGE
Green tree pythons, which live in northern Australia and New Guinea, are bright yellow or brick brown when they hatch. They become the green color of adults in one to three years.

ON THEIR OWN
Although some female snakes protect their eggs and keep them warm, they do not care for the newly hatched young. Once snakes hatch, they face many predators, including other snakes.

LIFE IN A COLD CLIMATE

Snakes that live in cool climates must seek shelter during the winter. They choose a dry place, such as a burrow or a crevice. Their metabolism slows down as the temperature drops, and this allows them to conserve their energy stores. Some cool climates may have such short warm seasons (when snakes are active) that the snakes can only gather enough energy to breed every two years.

Discover more in The Next Generation

Snakes on the Move

When snakes evolved from their lizard ancestors, they gradually lost their limbs—perhaps to take advantage of narrow spaces where limbs were not much use. Without limbs, however, snakes had to develop new ways of moving. Their longer, more supple bodies provided the solution. Instead of using legs, snakes lever themselves along on the edge of their belly scales, pushing with tiny muscles attached to the ribs. Snakes have developed four different ways to push their bodies along in their different habitats. Snakes move rapidly whether they are on land or in water by a process called lateral undulation. If they are in confined spaces, such as narrow crevices and tunnels, snakes use concertina movement (bunching the body together, then apart). Some heavy-bodied snakes use rectilinear (in a straight line) movement when they are moving slowly. Sidewinding movement is used only by a few snakes that live on loose, slippery surfaces, such as sand dunes.

LOW SPEEDS
Many heavy-bodied snakes, such as pythons and vipers, crawl in a straight line by pushing back with various sections of their belly while bringing other sections forward. This is called rectilinear movement.

ROWING IN THE WATER
Sea snakes and other water snakes move just like land snakes. Using lateral undulation, they push against the water with the sides of their curved bodies. Sea snakes have flattened tails to give them additional "push."

TRAVELING AT SPEED
With lateral undulation, a snake can move fast by pushing the side curves of its body against the surface it is traveling on or through. This anchor enables the snake to push forward.

CONCERTINA MOVEMENT
In a narrow space, a snake may anchor the front part of its body by pressing the coils against the sides of the space. It then draws up the rest of the body behind it. The snake anchors this part of the body and pushes the front part to a new anchor point.

DID YOU KNOW?

Snakes usually move at about 2 miles (3 km) per hour, and most species cannot "run" at more than 4 miles (7 km) per hour. The fastest reliable record is for an African black mamba, which moved at 7 miles (11 km) per hour over a distance of 141 ft (43 m).

GET A GRIP
Some tree snakes have a ridge running along the sides of their bellies. This helps them to take advantage of any knob on a branch or twig to push against in lateral undulation.

A WINDING ROAD
The sidewinder, a desert rattlesnake from North America, moves sideways across loose sand with only small sections of its body touching the hot ground at any one time. The snake anchors its head and tail in the sand and lifts its trunk off the ground, moving sideways. The head and tail then move into the same position.

GLIDING TO SAFETY

The flying tree snake can glide from one tree to another, or to the ground. Using lateral undulation, it launches itself into the air where it assumes a more or less straight position. Its belly is curved in, and acts like a parachute. These snakes probably use gliding as a way to escape birds or other predators in trees.

Discover more in Sizing up Snakes

Defense Tactics

A FRIGHTENING SIGHT
Like a frilled lizard, the harmless vine snake opens wide its brightly colored mouth to startle predators.

Most people fear snakes. We see them as deadly, cold-blooded killers, preying on all kinds of animals. But snakes are also preyed on. They are killed and eaten by fish, lizards, other snakes, birds of prey (snakes are a large part of the diet of some eagles, kingfishers and the Australian kookaburra) and mammals. Snakes have evolved a number of ways to defend themselves. Some rely on bright colors to let predators know they are venomous—there are harmless species that even mimic these colors! Others camouflage or bury themselves to hide from danger. Some snakes surprise their enemies by making themselves look bigger, hissing or lashing out with their bodies. Others keep perfectly still, as many predators depend on movement to find their prey. There are also snakes that rely on speed for escape, moving quickly into the cover of a burrow or up into a tree.

DEAD AND STINKING
The hog-nosed snake confuses predators by playing dead and refusing to move if it is touched. If a predator persists, the snake releases a foul smell.

PUMPED UP
If a twig snake is threatened by a predator, it suddenly inflates the loose skin on its chin and throat and makes itself look too big to attack.

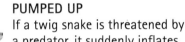

Venomous Mayan
coral snake

Non-venomous
false coral snake

FALSE COLORS
Some harmless snakes avoid predators by imitating venomous species. These two snakes live in the same region of Guatemala in Central America and look almost identical—they even have the same incomplete black bands! The only obvious difference is the red in the false coral snake's tail.

STRANGE BUT TRUE
The king snake is not venomous, but it hunts and eats venomous rattlesnakes! Strangely, rattlesnakes never make any attempt to defend themselves by biting their attackers.

PET TORTOISES

Tortoises used to be exploited for their meat and their shells. Today, tortoises are exploited as "pets." In some countries, they are now in danger of being crushed by cars and trail bikes. Tortoise habitats around the world are also being turned into agricultural land and housing subdivisions.

A PRECIOU...

People in m...
in specia...
decor...
ne...

DEADLY CAMOUFLAGE

The desert adder hides from predators and ambushes its prey by burying itself in the sand. Only its head and camouflaged eyes can be seen.

A TRICK OF THE EYE

Cobras and some other front-fanged venomous snakes flatten their necks to make themselves look bigger than they really are.

THE RATTLESNAKE'S RATTLE

The rattlesnake's famous rattle is made up of several interlocking horny segments that have the same structure as the horny scale at the tip of a "normal" snake's tail. When the snake vibrates its tail, the rattle segments move across each other to create a buzzing sound. This warns grazing animals that a rattlesnake is nearby. The natural curve of the segments lifts the rattle off the ground, which places it in the best position for making sounds and keeps it from becoming worn as the snake slides along the ground.

WARNING COLORS

A regal ring-necked snake displays its red-coiled tail to deter a predator. If the predator flips the snake over, it also sees the snake's orange belly. The colors orange and red signal danger to the predator.

Discover more in Snake Specifications

R

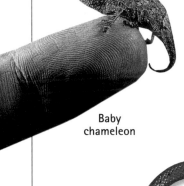

Pond turtle

Many reptiles arou[...] are endangered. [...] inconspicuous s[...] and snake are likely to b[...] during your lifetime, but [...] will probably not even [...] have gone. There are m[...] spectacular species, suc[...] crocodilians, large lizar[...] tortoises and sea turtles [...] also endangered. They [...] decline. Reptiles are th[...] their habitats are destr[...] cities and towns; wher[...] for meat, skins and otl[...] when they are collecte[...] when they are preyed [...] animals such as pigs, [...] mongooses and rats. [...] on islands or in other[...] especially vulnerable[...] occur in small numb[...] the main danger to [...] have the power to p[...] becoming extinct. W[...] control, all the activ[...] continue to endang[...]

A VALUABLE REPTILE
For many people living i[...] developing countries, a[...] or python skin can be w[...] month's wages. These p[...] native reptiles to help [...] standard of living.

Dwarf caiman

Baby chameleon

Coral snake

False coral snake

Horned chameleon

adaptation The way species of animals change to suit their environment.

ambush When animals hide (using their own camouflage, or by concealing themselves in bushes, in trees or beneath loose sand or soil), keep very still, then attack the surprised prey.

amphibians From the Greek meaning "two worlds." Amphibians (frogs, toads, axolotls, salamanders, caecilians and newts) are similar to reptiles, but they have moist skin and they lay their eggs in water.

amphisbaenians Burrowing, legless "worm lizards" found in Southeast Asia, Europe, the United States and Africa. Their heads are similar in shape to their tails, and their name means "going both ways."

ancestor A plant or animal from which a later form of plant or animal evolved.

aquatic Living most or all of the time in water.

camouflage When animals use colors and patterns that blend in with the background to conceal themselves from predators or to ambush prey.

carapace The upper or back part of a turtle or a tortoise's shell. The bottom part is called the plastron.

chelonian A turtle or tortoise. A member of the order Chelonia, one of the four major groups of reptiles.

chemoreceptors Small sensory organs in the mouth and nose that detect chemicals. Chemoreceptors are responsible for the senses of taste and smell.

cloaca The internal chamber in fish, amphibians, reptiles and birds into which the contents of the reproductive ducts and the waste ducts empty before being passed from the body.

cold-blooded An animal that cannot keep its body at more or less the same temperature by internal means. Reptiles are cold-blooded, but they control their body temperature by their behavior.

concertina locomotion A kind of movement used by some legless lizards and snakes in narrow passageways. The front of the body is extended forward, pressed against the sides of the walls, then the rest of the body is pulled forward.

crest A line of large, scaly spines on a lizard's neck and back. Many lizards can raise or lower their crests to communicate with other lizards.

crocodilian A crocodile, caiman, alligator, gharial or tomistoma. A member of the order Crocodilia.

dewlap A flap of skin, sometimes brightly colored, on a lizard's throat. Dewlaps usually lie close to the neck and can be extended to communicate with other lizards.

dinosaurs A group of reptiles that dominated Earth from the Triassic to the Cretaceous Period (245–65 million years ago). The largest land animals that ever lived, dinosaurs are more closely related to today's birds and crocodilians than they are to other living reptiles.

display Behavior, which can include showing brightly colored parts of the body, postures or actions, used to communicate threat, defense or readiness to mate.

diurnal Active during the day. Most reptiles are diurnal because they rely on the sun's heat to provide energy for hunting and other activities.

egg tooth A special scale on the tip of the upper lip of a hatchling lizard or snake. They use it to break a hole in the egg so the newborn animal can escape. The egg tooth falls off within a few days of hatching.

endangered animals Animals that are in danger of becoming extinct.

evolution When a population of plants or animals gradually changes its characteristics over generations so that it will have a better chance of surviving in an environment.

extinction The complete dying out of all members of a species.

flippers The broad front legs of sea turtles that act like paddles to "row" these animals through the water. Flippers are composed mainly of the bones of the fingers and hand.

fossil The preserved impression of a plant or an animal's body in rock, or evidence of an animal's activity, for example, footprints.

frill A collar around a frilled lizard's neck. Like a crest or dewlap, a frill can be raised to signal to other lizards or to surprise a predator.

62

gastroliths Stomach stones swallowed by crocodilians that stay in the stomach to help crush food.

habitat The place where an animal naturally lives.

hemotoxin A kind of venom produced by venomous snakes. Hemotoxic venom (the main chemical in the venom of vipers and rattlesnakes) destroys muscle tissue.

hibernate To remain inactive during the cold winter months. Some lizards and snakes that live in cold climates or in mountainous areas hibernate in burrows beneath the snow.

invertebrates Animals that do not have a backbone. Many have soft bodies (such as worms) or a hard shell (such as insects).

Jacobson's organ Two small sensory pits on the top part of the front of the mouth in lizards and snakes. They use this organ to analyze small molecules that they pick up from the air or ground and carry to the organ with the tongue.

keratin A material found in horns and fingernails.

lateral undulation A kind of movement used by legless lizards and snakes. Curves of the body push back against the rough ground and the animal moves forward through the curved path.

live-bearing Reptiles that do not lay eggs, but give birth to fully formed young.

nocturnal Active at night. Nocturnal animals sleep during the day. Most nocturnal reptiles become active shortly after the sun sets, taking advantage of the still-warm ground to raise their body temperature.

osteoderm A lump or nodule of bone in a reptile's skin that provides protection against predators. Most crocodilians and some lizards are protected by osteoderms as well as thick, strong skin.

pheromone A chemical that sends a signal to another member of the species. Reptiles produce pheromones to let others know they are ready to mate.

predator An animal that hunts and eats other animals.

pupil The round or slit-shaped opening in the center of the eye. Light passes through this to the back of the eye.

rectilinear locomotion A movement used by large snakes when moving slowly in a straight line. Small sections along the body push backwards against the ground while other small sections of the body are being pulled forwards to new positions.

reptile Cold-blooded vertebrates including tortoises, turtles, snakes, lizards and crocodilians.

rival An animal competing for food, territory and mates.

scales Distinct thick areas of a reptile's skin. Scales vary from being very small to large, and they may be smooth, keeled, spiny or granular.

scutes The horny plates that cover a chelonian's bony shell.

side-necked The way one group of chelonians draws the neck and head back under the shell by tucking the neck and head sideways under the rim of the shell.

straight-necked The way the other group of chelonians draws the neck and head straight back into the shell.

temperate When an environment or region has a warm (but not very hot) summer and a cool (but not very cold) winter.

terrestrial Living all or most of the time on land.

territory Area of land inhabited and defended by animals.

throat flap A valve at the back of a crocodilian's throat that closes to stop water from entering the trachea when eating prey underwater.

trachea The tube through which air passes to the lungs.

tropical A region near the equator that is warm to hot all year round. This kind of environment is ideal for cold-blooded reptiles.

venomous Describes animals that bite or sting, and deliver chemicals that can immobilise or kill prey or predators.

vertebrates Animals, for example, fishes, amphibians, reptiles, birds and mammals, which have backbones.

warm-blooded Able to keep the internal temperature of the body at a more or less stable temperature by internal means.

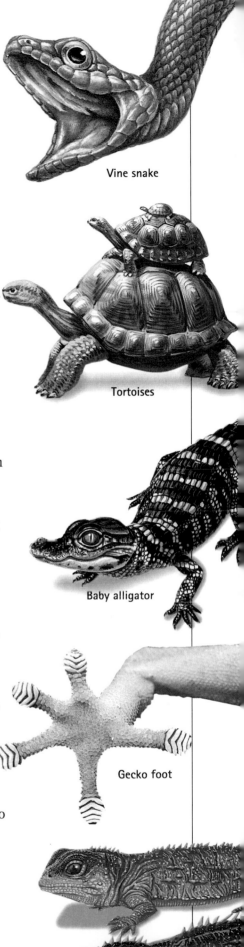

Vine snake

Tortoises

Baby alligator

Gecko foot

Tuataras

63

Index

Picture Credits

(t=top, b=bottom, l=left, r=right, c=center, F=front, C=cover, B=back, Bg=background)
Heather Angel, 61tr. **Ardea**, 10cl (H.D. Dossenbach), 38cl (F. Gohier), 58tr (P. Morris), 12c (W. Weisser), 47c (T. Willock). **Kathie Atkinson**, 17tl, 37br, 45cr. **Aurora**, 61c (J. Azel). **Auscape**, 23tr, 43br (Ferrero/Labat), 13cl (T. de Roy). **Austral International**, 53c (Shooting Star/A. Sirdofsky), 61cr (Sipa Press). **Australian Picture Library**, 47bc (G. Bell), 20cl (S. Osolinski). **Bruce Coleman Limited**, 30cr, 62bl (J. Burton), 21tr (A. Deane), 60tr (C.B. and D.W. Frith), 6cl (U. Hirsch), 19c (Jeff Foot Productions), 55bl (G. McCarthy), 15tl (S. Nielsen), 11tl (H. Reinhard), 14cl, 34bl, 59tl (A.J. Stevens), 32tl, 42br, 63bcr (J. Visser), 48cl (C. Zuber). **Michael and Patricia Fogden**, 18bc, 23tl, 31c, 36c, 39bl, 43tr, 45cl, 50cl, 50bcl, 50tcl, 57tl, 58/59b, 59tc. **Pavel German**, 32br, 35cr, 52tr. **The Image Bank**, 46bl (J.H. Carmichael, Jr.). **NHPA**, 54tc (A. Bannister), 14bl (J. Blossom), 52bl (J.H. Carmichael, Jr.), 43bl (S. Dalton), 6tr, 19bc (N.J. Dennis), 30tl, 35tc, 35tl, 37tr, 38br, 61br,
62cl (D. Heuclin), 54br (H. and V. Ingen), 48t (H. Palo Jr.), 22cl, 62tcl (J. Sauvanet). **North Wind Picture Archives**, 12bc. **Ocean Earth Images**, 56tr (K. Aitken). **Oxford Scientific Films**, 8tl, 23c (J. Downer), 9bl, 58cl (M. Fogden), 60/61c (F. Schneidermeyer), 28bl (K. Westerskov). **Planet Earth Pictures**, 22cr (J.B. Alker), 32bl, 36tr (M. Clay), 17cr (M. Conlin), 21tl (R. de la Harpe), 11tc (D.P. Maitland), 27cl (J. Scott), 60cr (J.D. Watt). **Michael Schneider**, 29bl (New Zealand Geographic). **South Australian Museum**, 29tr (S.C. Donnellan). **Oliver Strewe**, 60bl (Wave Productions). **Tom Stack & Associates**, 47bc (M. Bacon), 49tc (D.G. Barker), 11cr (M. Clay), 11tr, 59tr (K.T. Givens), 7tc, 10tr (T. Kitchin), 45c, 47tl, 51cl (J. McDonald), 8cr (K. Schafer). **John Visser**, 40tl, 41cr, 41tl. **Thomas A. Wiewandt**, 41tr, 47cr.

Illustration Credits

Anne Bowman, icons, 5cl, 5tl, 26br, 38bcl, 51tl. **Simone End**, 1, 3, 4/5b, 5br, 14tr, 15br, 15cr, 15tl, 16/17c, 16bl, 16c, 17tr, 22bl, 22tl, 22tr,
27tl, 30/31t, 30cl, 31t, 43cr, 48/49c, 48bc, 49tr, 50bl, 51tr, 58br, 58t, 63tr. **Christer Eriksson**, 14/15c, 23–26c, 27r, 42/43c, 50/51b, 50tl. **John Francis/Bernard Thornton Artists, UK**, 12cl, 12cr, 12tr, 13c, 38/39t, 38tl, 39br, 52/53b, 53cr, 53t, 63tcr. **Robert Hynes**, 8/9c, 8bc, 44/45b, 44/45t, 44bl, 44cl, 45tr. **David Kirshner**, 4/5t, 4l, 6/7c, 6bl, 7br, 7tl, 10/11b, 10/11c, 11br, 18/19t, 18br, 19r, 20/21b, 20tr, 30b, 35tr, 40/41b, 40cl, 41cl, 49tl, 58bl, 62bcl, 62tl, 63cr. **Frank Knight**, 6tl, 54/55t, 54tl, 55br. **James McKinnon**, 28/29c, 28br, 28c, 63br. **Colin Newman/Bernard Thornton Artists, UK**, 32/33t, 32cl, 33cl, 33b, 33r, 36/37c, 36bl. **Trevor Ruth**, 2l, 46/47c, 47br, 47tr, 56/57c, 56bl, 56t, 57br. **Peter Schouten**, 34/35c, 34tr, 60/61b. **Rod Westblade**, endpapers.

Cover Credits

Bruce Coleman Limited, BCtl. **Simone End**, BCbr. **Christer Eriksson**, FCc, FCtr. **David Kirshner**, FCtl. **The Photo Library, Sydney**, Bg (TSI/Tim Davis).